SOCIAL EMOTIONAL LEARNING WORKBOOK FOR MIDDLE SCHOOL

Navigating Emotions with Grade Level Activities

Richard Bass

2 Free Bonuses

Receive a **FREE** Planner for Kids and a copy of the Positive Discipline Playbook by scanning below!

Contents

Exploring Career Paths

Part 1: Basic Information

Career Title

Sector

Job Description

Average Starting Salary

Part 2: Education & Training

Majors in High School (if applicable)

Minimum Level of Education Required (e.g., high school diploma or bachelor's degree)

Additional Training, Licenses, or Certifications

Typical Career Progression (e.g. junior, specialist, or managerial opportunities)

Part 3: Skills & Qualities

Key Skills

Personal Qualities

Part 4: Work Environment

Work Setting

Typical Work Hours

Work-Life Balance

Potential Challenges

My Resumé

Contact Information

Summary

Education

Experience

Skills

Interests/Hobbies:

My Personal Budget

My Financial Goal

Tracking My Income and Expenses

Monthly Income

Monthly Expenses

Budget Summary

Savings Allocation

Notes and Adjustments

My Personal SWOT Analysis

My Future Decision

Strengths

Weaknesses

Opportunities

Introduction

Gaining Confidence, One Skill at a Time

The only person you should try to be better than is the person you were yesterday.
- Matty Mullins

Jaden, a bright sixth-grader, struggled with social challenges, feeling self-conscious due to his voice, which was quieter compared to his peers. He often took a back seat in group projects, felt anxious about presentations, and usually stayed close to his best friend at recess. When his friend was absent, Jaden spent recess alone.

Noticing these issues, Jaden's teacher, informed by a recent social-emotional learning workshop, proposed a plan. Over 30 weeks, she organized weekly hour-long sessions with Jaden, incorporating interactive social-emotional activities and discussions. Jaden's parents supported this, and he eagerly participated. By the end of the year, Jaden's social skills and confidence had significantly improved. He learned to view his small voice as a unique trait, made new friends who shared his interests, and set personal and academic goals.

Many students face similar challenges such as managing emotions, making friends, or sharing their thoughts confidently. The *Social Emotional Learning Workbook for Middle School* addresses these issues with interactive activities tailored for sixth, seventh, and eighth graders. With 30 activities per grade level, the workbook aims to equip students with essential social-emotional skills, enhancing their middle school experience and building a foundation for lifelong emotional intelligence and resilience.

 ## Overview of Social-Emotional Learning

Social-emotional learning (SEL) is a teaching method developed by the US-based organization CASEL, which promotes the development of students' social, academic, and emotional competencies (CASEL, n.d.). SEL involves acquiring and applying social and emotional skills to enhance students' attitudes, behaviors, and healthy identities. It encourages empathy, positive decision-making, and improved peer relationships, making classroom interactions more enjoyable and memorable. Beyond the classroom, SEL empowers students to care for their communities, from random acts of kindness to planning community projects, helping them set collective goals and make responsible decisions.

Implementing SEL in the classroom can boost students' social skills, constructive behaviors, and academic performance. Research indicates that SEL practices lead to higher grades, better test scores, increased homework completion, and improved attendance due to enhanced student engagement (Cipriano et al., 2023). Additionally, SEL programs reduce emotional distress and discipline problems while fostering positive behaviors toward the self and others (Durlak et al., 2022).

The five core competencies of SEL that will be presented in this workbook are as follows:

1. **Self-awareness:** Recognizing and understanding your emotions and how they impact your attitudes and behaviors.
2. **Self-management:** Practicing self-control and making the right choices in different social situations.
3. **Social awareness:** Being mindful and empathetic toward the perspectives and circumstances of others, including people who come from diverse cultural backgrounds.
4. **Relationship skills:** Using effective communication and social skills to build and maintain healthy relationships that feel satisfying and supportive.
5. **Responsible decision-making:** Making careful and considerate decisions about personal behaviors during various social situations such as group work and conflict resolution.

For Students: How to Get the Most Out of This Workbook

As you go through the workbook, start with activities that have been added under your grade level. If you have time and wish to gain more practice, feel free to explore the activities added under the other grade levels. Approach each activity with curiosity and honesty, reflecting on your experiences and sharing insights with your classmates or teachers, if you are comfortable.

Many of these activities can be completed at school during class time. If you need extra time to complete any of the activities, ask your teacher if you can continue to work on the activities at home. The best part about this workbook is that sections and activities can be torn out for greater convenience. This also ensures that the workbook stays at school rather than going home with you.

Some activities may require you to work with different classmates in pairs or groups. Through teamwork, you can share ideas and thoughts about the skills you are learning and walk away with richer knowledge. If you struggle to complete any of the activities, reach out to your classmates, teachers, parents, or school counselor, if needed.

This workbook aims to empower you to succeed in different social contexts and become the best student and individual that you can be. Get ready to explore the world of SEL through awesome activities that will both challenge and inspire you for the rest of the school year!

Chapter - 1

Sixth Grade-Building Self-Awareness to Gain Confidence

To be nobody but yourself in a world which is doing its best, night and day, to make you everybody else - means to fight the hardest battle which any human being can fight; and never stop fighting.

- E. E. Cummings

 What Is Self-Awareness?

Have you heard about the concept of self-awareness? It can be described as the ability to understand your thoughts, feelings, and behaviors and how they influence your relationships with others. Strengthening your self-awareness helps you connect the dots about why you think certain thoughts, feel certain emotions, or make certain choices. Armed with this knowledge, you can then develop a stronger connection to yourself and improve the way you interact with others.

Imagine how different your classroom experiences would be if you could anticipate what would happen if you behaved in certain ways. Self-awareness is a superpower that allows you to identify your strengths and weaknesses, allowing you to make choices that build confidence and bring out the best version of yourself.

When you feel disappointed about not performing as well as you wanted to on a test, self-awareness helps you tune into your emotions, minimize negative thinking, and find ways to cheer yourself up and get back on track. Being self-aware helps you tackle new and unique challenges that you are presented with in middle school with more patience, curiosity, and a positive attitude!

 30 Weeks of Fun: Self-Awareness and Confidence-Building Activities for Sixth-Grade Students

When was the last time you took a moment to think about how your thoughts, feelings, and behaviors impact your classroom interactions and academic performance? The following SEL activities have been created to help you strengthen your self-awareness, transforming the way you express who you are around others and how you confront challenging school situations.

 Activity 1: Personal Strengths Cards

Possessing certain strengths can make completing class tasks easier and help you feel more connected to your classmates. Personal Strengths Cards is designed to help you discover these strengths and show how they can make your school life more rewarding.

Here's what you need to do: First, identify your personal strengths by answering the questions below. Then, decorate the blank personal strength cards to showcase these strengths. On each card, write down a personal strength and draw a symbol or picture that represents it.

Once your cards are ready, pair up with a classmate and play a game of matching cards. One person starts by placing a personal strength card on the table. The other person looks through their deck of cards to find a strength that matches the one on the table. Keep going until you've found matches for all your strengths. This game shows how your strengths can benefit others and make your relationships more fulfilling.

Personal strength questions:

1. What school tasks or activities are you good at? These should be things that come naturally to you without putting in a lot of effort.

_____

_____

_____

_____

_____

2. What school subjects do you enjoy the most and look forward to?

3. Reflect on moments at school when you felt proudest of yourself. What did you accomplish?

_____

_____

_____

_____

_____

_____

_____

_____

4. What do your teachers and classmates normally compliment you about? What positive comments do you hear often from them?

_____

_____

_____

_____

_____

_____

_____

_____

_____

_____

_____

_____

_____

5. In what ways do you show support to your classmates? What are your best ways to offer help to others?

_____

_____

_____

_____

_____

_____

_____

_____

_____

_____

6. When do you feel happiest at school? What activities bring out that excitement? Note that these don't have to be activities related to classwork.

_____

_____

_____

_____

_____

_____

_____

_____

_____

_____

_____

7. In your opinion, what behaviors and qualities do you display that make you a good friend? List them below.

_____

_____

_____

_____

_____

_____

_____

_____

_____

_____

Based on the responses written above, take a moment to think about your personal strengths-the abilities you have that set you apart from other students and make you feel happy and engaged at school. In each card, write down a personal strength and draw a symbol or picture to represent it. Be creative and go wild when decorating your cards.

MY PERSONAL STRENGTH IS _____

MY PERSONAL STRENGTH IS _____

MY PERSONAL STRENGTH IS _____

MY PERSONAL STRENGTH IS _____

MY PERSONAL STRENGTH IS _____

MY PERSONAL STRENGTH IS --

MY PERSONAL STRENGTH IS --

15

MY PERSONAL STRENGTH IS --

MY PERSONAL STRENGTH IS --

17

MY PERSONAL STRENGTH IS --

Activity 2: Strengths and Weaknesses Map

A treasure map is a creative guide that helps you locate hidden treasure with clues and warnings to avoid traps and choose the right paths. Think of the Strengths and Weaknesses Map as your personal treasure map for achieving school goals. By using your strengths and navigating around your weaknesses, you can ensure success without falling into traps.

Use the *Strengths and Weaknesses Map* page at the end of the chapter to create your own map. Here's what to include:

1. **Draw your goal:** It could be improving grades, participating more in class, or meeting homework deadlines.
2. **Draw paths for strengths and weaknesses:** For example, studying the day before a test leads to a dead-end, while asking for help brings you closer to success.
3. **Create an action plan:** Use your strengths to your advantage and find ways around your weaknesses. For every dead-end, provide an alternative route.
4. **Mark checkpoints:** Track your progress and see how close you are to reaching your goal.

Activity 3: Using Personal Strengths to Overcome Setbacks

Whenever you are feeling discouraged at school due to the increased workload or expectations, spend some time thinking about ways where you can use your personal strengths to improve the situation. You could have special skills or talents that can make completing school work or handling stressful situations much easier.

For this activity, refer to the personal strengths you identified in Activity 1. Write them down in a list below.

_____

_____

_____

_____

_____

_____

_____

_____

_____

_____

_____

For each personal strength, think of at least three challenging situations it can help you with. For example, if you are naturally good with numbers, you can
- *solve complicated math sums.*
- *keep track of time when working on your assignments.*
- *memorize due dates and submissions for school work.*

If you enjoy telling jokes, you can
- *use humor to make friends.*
- *cheer up your classmates when they are feeling down.*
- *cheer yourself up when you are feeling down.*

Use the same format to recognize the ways in which your personal strengths can bring you out of uncomfortable situations.

_____

_____

_____

_____

_____

_____

_____

_____

_____

_____

_____

_____

Activity 4: Goal-Setting Basics

To become the best version of yourself, you will need to regularly set goals and work toward accomplishing them. Goal-setting is a fun and structured way of establishing goals. The SMART framework is a simple form of goal-setting that you can use to outline your goals.

SMART stands for specific, measurable, attainable, relevant, and time-bound. These five steps walk you through creating clear and actionable goals. Below is a challenge to help you establish your first SMART goal.

Specific: _Clearly state something that you would like to achieve at school. For example, "To improve my confidence in sharing my thoughts during class discussions."_

_____

_____

_____

_____

_____

_____

Measurable: Identify a number, percentage, or another quantity that you can use to measure your progress. For example, "Raising my hand at least once during class discussions so that I can share my thoughts."

_____

_____

_____

_____

_____

_____

_____

_____

_____

Attainable: Read over your goal and make sure it is something you can realistically achieve. For example, "Yes, I am capable of raising my hand at least once during class discussions."

_____

_____

_____

_____

_____

_____

_____

_____

Relevant: Make sure that the goal you set is what you deeply want and not something your parents, teachers, or classmates might want for you. For example, "My goal to participate more in class discussions is something I want because it can boost my confidence and help me engage with my classmates."

_____

_____

_____

_____

_____

_____

_____

_____

Time-bound: Set a reasonable deadline for when you expect to achieve your goal. For example, "I am giving myself three months to gain confidence in sharing my thoughts during class discussions."

_____

_____

_____

_____

_____

_____

_____

_____

Activity 5: Creating Attitude Goals Using the SMART Framework

In the previous activity, you learned the steps for structuring your goals using the SMART goal-setting framework. In this activity, your task is to apply the same steps to create an attitude goal, which is a goal related to your moods and emotions at school or home.

Below are the five steps that you can follow.

Specific: *Clearly state the attitude adjustment you would like to see at school or home. For example, "I want to become more patient with my younger sibling."*

_____

_____

_____

_____

_____

_____

_____

_____

_____

_____

Measurable: *Identify a number, percentage, or another quantity that you can use to measure your progress. For example, "To become more patient with my younger sibling, I will count up to 10 slowly when I feel like yelling at them."*

_____

_____

_____

_____

_____

_____

Attainable: Read over your goal and make sure it is something you can realistically achieve. For example, "Yes, I am capable of counting up to 10 slowly."

_____

_____

_____

_____

_____

_____

_____

_____

_____

Relevant: Make sure that the goal you set is what you deeply want and not something your parents, teachers, or classmates might want for you. For example, "My goal to be more patient with my sibling is something I want because it can help us build a positive relationship and stop fighting with each other."

_____

_____

_____

_____

_____

_____

_____

_____

Time-bound: *Set a reasonable deadline for when you expect to achieve your goal. For example, "I am giving myself two months to work on achieving this goal."*

_____

_____

_____

_____

_____

_____

_____

_____

_____

_____

Activity 6: Finding an Accountability Buddy

Sharing your goals with someone you trust can boost your chances of success. An accountability buddy-this could be a classmate, friend, or parent-understands your goals and offers support and encouragement to keep you on track. Look for a buddy who is kind, patient, committed, and honest, and who understands your goal enough to give useful advice.

Your task is to interview three people from your circle of friends and family to find the best accountability buddy. Use the interview questions below to learn about each candidate, then choose the one who makes you feel the most supported and motivated.

Interview Questions:

1. *How do you manage disappointment and challenges?*
2. *What do you believe is the most important quality for achieving goals?*
3. *What type of support can you offer to help me achieve my goals?*
4. *How would you keep me motivated if I started to slack on my goals?*
5. *How often do you expect me to update you on my progress?*

Activity 7: Drawing the Best Version of Me

Sometimes, you need to be reminded of what the best version of yourself looks like in order to stay motivated to improve your habits. For this activity, you are required to get your coloring pencils out and turn to the blank page at the end of the chapter titled "Drawing the Best Version of Me." There, you will find space to draw the best version of yourself.

You can decide what attributes to highlight. A good tip is to reflect on some of your personal goals. For example, if one of your personal goals is to get a healthy body, you can draw yourself playing sports or exercising. If your goal is to discover new hobbies, you can draw yourself engaging in different activities. There are no right or wrong ways to perform this activity. Draw what feels meaningful for you!

 ## Activity 8: Positive Self-Talk to Counter Critical Thoughts

Do you ever catch yourself thinking things like, "I'm not as smart as everyone else," or "I'll probably mess up on that test"? Those thoughts can cloud your mind and make it seem like reaching your goals is impossible. It's true that not everything will work out perfectly the first time, but that doesn't mean you can't succeed.

One way to fight these negative thoughts is through positive self-talk–a powerful technique that changes how you talk to yourself. Positive self-talk helps you focus on the good parts of your school life, friendships, or home situation instead of dwelling on the bad. It teaches you to appreciate the things that are going well and stay hopeful about areas where you want to improve.

To practice positive self-talk, try turning negative statements into positive and hopeful ones. For example, instead of thinking, "I never get picked first for the team," you could say, "Whether I'm chosen first or last, I'm grateful for the chance to play with my friends." Do the same for the statements below.

Negative statements	Positive statements
I always embarrass myself whenever I get up to speak in front of the class.	
Science is difficult. I will never understand it.	

Nobody ever asks me to attend their birthday parties.	
I'll never be as good at baseball as my friend.	
I can never seem to complete my tests on time.	
I'll never become an A student no matter how hard I try.	
I feel left out when I hear my friends talking about a topic I don't understand.	
I always say the wrong things when I attempt to share my feelings.	
I'm not as popular as the other kids in my class.	
I hate school. I wish I didn't have to be here.	

Activity 9: "Thank You" Jar

Helping others is a great way to boost your self-esteem and feel good about yourself. It also reminds you of your strengths. For instance, when a classmate thanks you for helping them with something, it shows how good you are at explaining things.

Here's a cool idea to encourage more kindness at school: Bring an empty, clear mason jar to school. Take off the paper cover so you can see inside. Write your name on the lid with a marker. Your teacher will set up a spot for your jar. Whenever you do something nice for a classmate, they can write a thank-you note on paper and put it in your jar. If someone helps you out, tear off a piece of paper, write a thank-you note, and put it in their jar.

It might take a while for your jar to fill up, so be patient. In the meantime, you can read the notes inside your jar and see how your kindness has made a difference.

 ## Activity 10: Clarifying Core Values

Core values are the principles that set the tone for your life and shed light on what you are passionate about, how you expect others to treat you, and what type of goals you strive for. Being aware of your core values helps you make better choices at school and home that match your desires and goals. For example, if you value support, you can make more of an effort to ask for help and receive the support you need.

There are a few steps that you can go through to explore your core values:

- Make a list of the things that matter most in your school life. Use the table below as inspiration to come up with your list.

Honesty	Teamwork	Support	Doing your best
Respect	Responsibility	Compassion	Encouragement
Creativity	Playfulness	Learning	Pursuing Goals
Challenges	Adventure	Equality	Being included
Hardwork	Friendship	Balance	Leadership
Achievement	Acceptance	Praise and Recognition	Learning from mistakes

_____

_____

_____

_____

_____

_____

_____

_____

_____

_____

_____

- Narrow down your list to five values and write them in the order of their importance, starting with the most important value.

_____

_____

_____

_____

_____

_____

_____

_____

_____

_____

- For each value, write down examples of how you can honor it. Think of practical ways to demonstrate these values every time you are at school.

_____

_____

_____

_____

_____

_____

_____

_____

_____

_____

- Make a list of the people who can help you develop your values. For example, if you value hard work, perhaps you can speak to your teacher and arrange extra lessons or exercises you can practice at home to improve your knowledge about the subject. If you value teamwork, you can speak to your extracurricular coaches about joining a social club or sports team.

_____

_____

_____

_____

_____

_____

_____

_____

Activity 11: Envision Your Goals

Constantly thinking about your goals is great. However, what happens during days or weeks when you forget what you are working toward?

A vision board is a creative reminder of your goals, which you can hang up in your bedroom or slip inside your homework diary (if it is small enough). It consists of photo and word cutouts that you can source from a magazine, displaying the goals that you're currently working on or goals that you aspire to achieve in the future. The aim is to see your desired outcomes and be reminded each day that you are getting closer to making them a reality.

Follow these simple instructions to create your vision board:

1. *Collect old magazines that explore topics relevant to your interests and passions.*
2. *Cut out both images and words from the magazines. Use a pair of scissors and trace the images and words neatly.*
3. *Arrange your cutouts on paper and create a collage where the images and words overlap without leaving any gaps.*
4. *Once you are satisfied, glue the cutouts on the paper and allow it to dry.*

 ## *Activity 12: Famous Wise Words*

Whenever you need a boost to remind yourself of what you're capable of achieving, turn to inspiring quotes from people who've accomplished amazing things. Take Thomas Edison, who invented the light bulb after trying 1,000 times, or Amelia Earhart, the first woman to fly solo across the Atlantic. Their words can encourage you to believe in yourself and keep pushing forward even when unexpected challenges arise.

For this activity, your goal is to find 10 quotes from famous figures. Look for quotes that cover different topics like overcoming fear, achieving success, setting goals, building self-confidence, and embracing change. When you face self-doubt and need a lift, revisit these quotes. Remember the hurdles these remarkable people overcame to reach their dreams. Let their courage inspire you to face challenges head-on and believe in your own potential!

 ## *Activity 13: Accomplishment Timeline*

Time flies when you are busy at school. However, every once in a while, it's important to stop time and reflect on past accomplishments to see how far you have come. The Accomplishment Timeline is an activity that will take you back in time so you can track your school progress.

On the blank page titled "Accomplishment Timeline" that can be found at the end of the chapter, draw a horizontal line with a ruler and add small marks after every 3-5 centimeters. Those marks represent milestones that you have reached from elementary to middle school. You can decide how many milestones to record. The size of the milestones doesn't matter, as long as it's something that makes you feel proud.

Tear out your timeline and place it somewhere safe. In six months' time, refer back to it and see what new milestones you can add. Keep on adding and documenting your milestones to track your progress.

 ## Activity 14: My Favorite Memories Book

School is about gaining skills and knowledge; but in between the focus and learning, there are positive memories that you make inside and outside of the classroom. My Favorite Memories Book is an activity that helps you capture these memories. Imagine having a book filled with all the hilarious and unforgettable things that happen at school, like that weird moment in class or that epic game you played during recess.

To create a memories book, you will need an A5 notebook that is specifically used for recording the wild and hilarious memories you make at school. You can keep the notebook in your school bag for easy access. Whenever something new occurs, write it down in your notebook. Include details like the date, location, and the event.

Here's an example:

> 10th December 2023
> Location: Classroom
> Event: Mr. Smith accidentally turned on the disco lights during math class!
> Everyone started dancing instead of solving equations.

 ## Activity 15: Personal Success Stories

Personal success stories remind you of how strong and capable you are while inspiring listeners to keep a positive mindset. These are stories that start out sad or worrying, then, through problem-solving and seeking guidance, end on a happy and successful note.

Every great personal success story has three sections:

1. **The dilemma:** Something awful happens that leaves you feeling sad or confused.
2. **Problem-solving and exploration:** You brainstorm ways to get yourself out of the situation and experiment with different solutions until one of them ends up working.

3. The turnaround moment: After implementing the solution, your situation takes a positive turn and you feel a sense of relief.

Using the same structure, create your personal success story, then get into groups or sit in a circle with your classmates and share your stories. Clap for each person after they have shared their story.

_____

_____

_____

_____

_____

_____

_____

_____

_____

_____

_____

_____

_____

_____

_____

_____

_____

_____

_____

_____

_____

Activity 16: Daily Wins and Losses

You will experience both good and bad events at school. These can be referred to as your daily wins and losses. Daily wins include things like finishing your homework in class, being complimented by your teacher, or contributing to class discussions. On the other hand, daily losses include things like arriving late for class, being reprimanded by your teacher, or receiving test scores that you weren't expecting.

Recording your daily wins and losses allows you to keep track of how you are performing at school and what you possibly need help with. For instance, if you record more wins than losses, see it as an opportunity to set challenging goals and push yourself to achieve more. If you record more losses than wins, perhaps it's time to approach your teacher and seek help.

To help you get the hang of recording your daily wins and losses, fill out the following table for a week. Afterward, continue the exercise in your homework diary or a separate notebook.

	Monday	Tuesday	Wednesday	Thursday	Friday
Daily Wins					
Daily Losses					

 Activity 17: Mind Mapping Interests and Hobbies

What are some of your interests and hobbies? Can you name them? Interests are things that you are curious about and seek to explore deeply. They could be school subjects, specific skills like learning a language, or sports and cultural competitions. Hobbies are activities that get you excited and energized. These could be activities that are fun and adventurous, activities that you are good at, or activities that help you relax.

This activity helps you map out your interests and hobbies so you can discover things that you already know about yourself, as well as some things that you didn't know about yourself. Here's what to do:

- Turn to the blank page at the end of the chapter titled "Mind Mapping Interests and Hobbies."

- Write "My Interests and Hobbies" in the center of the page and draw a circle around it.
- Draw four lines coming out from the circle in different directions.
- At the end of each line, write down an interest or hobby you have and circle them.
- For each interest or hobby, draw two more lines out from it and jot down other things that are like it or that you might enjoy.
- Keep going until you've listed as many interests and hobbies as you can think of.
- Use a highlighter to mark any interests or hobbies that surprise you or that you didn't realize you were into.

 ## Activity 18: Mistakes Journal

Making mistakes is not the end of the world. In fact, it is the beginning of learning. Mistakes offer you a chance to gain more information from your actions so you can make better choices next time. Learning from mistakes requires asking yourself tough questions about what went wrong and what you can do differently moving forward.

Whenever you encounter challenges and make mistakes, take a few minutes to journal about your experience with your mistakes journal. Go through the following five questions each time:

1. What went wrong?
2. Why did it happen?
3. What weaknesses did my mistake reveal?
4. What strengths can I use next time to avoid the mistake?
5. What type of support do I need?

Use an example of a recent mistake you made in the past week or month and answer the five questions below.

_____

_____

_____

_____

_____

_____

_____

_____

_____

_____

_____

_____

_____

_____

_____

_____

_____

_____

_____

_____

_____

_____

_____

_____

_____

_____

_____

Activity 19: Growth Mindset Crossword Puzzle

A growth mindset is the belief that you can develop your skills and become a better version of yourself over time. To adopt this mindset, you need to see failure as a stepping stone to achieve your goals and not as a sign to quit. You are capable of accomplishing victories at school and in your personal life, if you only keep going!

Here is a fun and relaxing crossword puzzle that will introduce you to terms related to a growth mindset. You are welcome to complete the puzzle in pairs or groups for support.

Test your knowledge by filling in the crossword puzzle below. When you're done, check your answers at the end of the chapter on Page (66)

Across:

2. A difficult situation that isn't easy to solve.

5. Bouncing back from setbacks and continuing to try.

6. Information about your performance that helps you improve.

8. The process of developing and improving over time.

10. Continuing to try, even after experiencing failure.

Down:

1. The ability to keep going, even when things are tough.

3. Errors made during learning that provide valuable lessons.

4. Your attitudes and beliefs about your abilities and potential.

7. The hard work you put into learning and improving.

9. The process of acquiring knowledge or skills.

Activity 20: Dear Future Me

Write a letter to your future self-the person you hope to become two, three, or five years from now. Share your hopes and dreams as well as fears that you may have about growing up. Consider the positive changes you would like to see in different areas of your life, such as your schooling, friendships, health and fitness, hobbies and interests, family relationships, career and life after school, and so on.

You can choose to either write out your letter in the blank page provided at the end of the chapter titled "Dear Future Me," or type out your letter and save it on your computer. Refer to your letter whenever you are feeling nervous about the future so you can remind yourself of your exciting plans.

 ## Activity 21: My Passion Project

A passion project is a task that you undertake purely for the love of what you are doing. It isn't supposed to be stressful or something that can be graded. It is only meant to bring joy and satisfy your curiosity. This activity will help you get started on your passion project. Take as much time as you need and don't forget to share photos and progress updates with your teachers and classmates along the way. Here are the guidelines to follow when getting started with your passion project:

1. *Refer to the hobbies and interests from Activity 17.*
2. *Choose one interest and set a goal using the SMART framework from Activity 4.*
3. *Learn about the process, materials, skills, and time required, and find useful resources like websites or YouTube channels.*
4. *Set a deadline; break the goal into smaller tasks; decide how many hours per week to dedicate; and schedule your time.*
5. *Document your progress, obstacles, mistakes (and lessons learned), and interesting knowledge gained.*
6. *Show your work to friends and family and seek constructive feedback to improve your project.*

 ## Activity 22: THINK Before You Speak

Words are like toothpaste squeezed out of a tube-once they're out, you can't put them back in. That's why it's crucial to think before you speak and consider how your words might affect others. One way to do this is by using the acronym THINK, which stands for True, Helpful, Inspiring, Necessary, and Kind. Before you say something, ask yourself these five questions:

1. *Is it true?*
2. *Is it helpful?*
3. *Is it inspiring?*
4. *Is it necessary?*
5. *Is it kind?*

Only share your message if you can answer "yes" to all these questions.

Now, let's practice using THINK. Look at the statements below and assess them using the five criteria to see if they meet all, some, or none of the THINK standards.

1. **Statement:** "You did a great job on your presentation! I learned a lot."

_____

_____

_____

_____

_____

_____

_____

_____

2. **Statement:** "Why are you always so slow at finishing your work?"

_____

_____

_____

_____

_____

_____

_____

_____

_____

_____

_____

3. Statement: "I heard that Jake got in trouble for cheating on the test."

_____

_____

_____

_____

_____

_____

_____

_____

_____

_____

4. Statement: "I'm really proud of you for standing up for what you believe in."

_____

_____

_____

_____

_____

_____

_____

_____

_____

_____

_____

_____

_____

5. Statement: "That shirt looks awful on you."

_____

_____

_____

_____

_____

_____

_____

_____

_____

_____

_____

_____

_____

_____

_____

_____

_____

_____

Activity 23: Compliment Chain

Everybody has a special quality that makes them stand out from the crowd! In this activity, you are required to help your classmates discover their special qualities by giving them a compliment.

To get started, sit or stand in a circle. One person starts by looking at the classmate to their right and giving them a compliment. It could be related to their academic performance, athletic abilities, unique personality, or how they treat others. The person who receives the compliment should say thank you, then turn to the person on their right and compliment them. Keep going until everyone in the circle has received a compliment.

After the activity, return to your desk and journal about the compliment that you received. Here are a few questions to help you reflect:

- How did the compliment make you feel?
- Was the compliment a surprise or something you have heard before?
- What strengths does the compliment reveal about you?
- How can you use your unique qualities to continue positively impacting others?

 ## Activity 24: My Circle of Control

Things won't always go as planned, but don't panic. Focus on what you can control and let go of what you can't. *My Circle of Control* helps you identify what you can change and what is out of your hands. For instance, while you can't change the test date, you can adjust your study routine to prepare better.

On the blank page provided within the My Circle of Control chapter, you'll find a large circle. Inside it, write down school-related things you can control, such as
- arriving on time to class
- greeting classmates
- choosing who to hang out with during recess

Outside the circle, write down things you can't control, like
- what classmates say about you
- assignment deadlines and test dates
- classroom rules and school policies

After completing your circle, focus on what you can't control. For each statement, think of a positive action to ease your anxiety. Start with, "I can't change [situation out of your control], but I can [positive action]." For example, "I can't change the test questions, but I can make study notes and practice different exercises every day."

Activity 25: Creating Your Study Timetable

A common task that students dread is studying for upcoming tests and exams. Having to sit down for several minutes or hours and learn large amounts of information can be overwhelming. However, with the right study timetable, you can enjoy stress-free study sessions that leave you feeling confident rather than drained.

The secret to acing tests and exams is to have a well-structured study timetable that you follow during the days and weeks leading up to the assessment. When creating your study timetable, here's what you need to do:

1. Create a list of the subjects you need to study and the topics you will be assessed on under each subject.

Example: English
- *phrases and clauses*
- *figurative language*
- *parts of speech*
- *comprehension skills*

2. After you have created your subject lists, rank each topic item on a scale of 1-10 to determine how much you currently understand (1 means no understanding and 10 means a very strong understanding).

Example: English
- *phrases and clauses: 6/10*
- *figurative language: 5.5/10*
- *parts of speech: 8/10*
- *comprehension skills: 7/10*

Based on the rankings, you can identify topics that need more focus. These topics will be allocated more time and practiced more than once per week.

The next step is to create a weekly timetable. Create a simple table with the days of the week as column headings and your subjects as side headings. It should look like this:

	Monday	Tuesday	Wednesday	Thursday	Friday
English					

1. Decide on the best time of day for you to study. Do you prefer the mornings before school or afternoons when you return home? Once you have figured that out, choose between a 1-hour study session or a 2-hour study session (you can switch study sessions for different days).

2. Split your study session among each subject topic, allocating time for each. Do not exceed 30 minutes for each topic. Also, make sure the topics that you are least confident about get more time than the others.

Example: 2-hour session
English

- *phrases and clauses: 25 minutes*
- *figurative language: 30 minutes*
- *parts of speech: 15 minutes*
- *comprehension skills: 20 minutes*

Total time: 90 minutes (or 1.5 hours).

1. Allocate study breaks in between each item on your agenda. The duration of your study breaks will depend on how much time you have remaining. In our example, we chose a 2-hour session and allocated 90 minutes for studying, leaving us with 30 minutes for study breaks. Insert a study break after going through each topic.

Example: 2-hour session
English

- *phrases and clauses: 25 minutes*
- *study break: 10 minutes*
- *figurative language: 30 minutes*
- *study break: 10 minutes*
- *parts of speech: 15 minutes*
- *study break: 10 minutes*
- *comprehension skills: 20 minutes*

Total time: 120 minutes (or 2 hours).

2. The final step is to add your agenda to your weekly timetable. Remember, each subject on your study list will have a different agenda depending on the topics covered, study session length, and number of breaks taken. The final outcome should look like this:

	Monday
English	**English (Afternoon)** • Phrases and clauses: 25 minutes • Study break: 10 minutes • Figurative language: 30 minutes • Study break: 10 minutes • Parts of speech: 15 minutes • Study break: 10 minutes • Comprehension skills: 20 minutes **Total time: 120 minutes (or 2 hours).**

 ## Activity 26: I Feel, I Need

Sometimes, you need to stand up for yourself and let others know how their actions affect you and what you need from them to feel safe. For instance, if you're not comfortable with classmates hugging you, it's important to tell them how hugs make you feel and suggest an alternative. The I Feel, I Need activity will help you set healthy boundaries with classmates, friends, and anyone who might make you upset or uncomfortable.

Using this statement is simple. First, explain how the behavior makes you feel (like hurt, annoyed, awkward, or left out). Then, say what you want them to do instead. Here are some examples:

- I feel uncomfortable when you hug me. I need you to give me a high-five or a fist bump instead.
- I feel annoyed when you take my things without asking. I need you to ask for permission before using my stuff.
- I feel stressed when you pressure me to join activities I'm not interested in. I need you to respect my decision when I say no.

Go through the scenarios below and consider what you would say to set boundaries. Remember to use "I feel, I need" statements.

1. Scenario: Your sibling is playing loud music during your study time.

_____

_____

_____

_____

_____

_____

_____

_____

2. Scenario: Your classmate teases you about your physical appearance.

_____

_____

_____

_____

_____

_____

_____

_____

_____

_____

3. Scenario: You catch your classmate copying your homework.

_____
_____
_____
_____
_____
_____
_____
_____
_____
_____

4. Scenario: You are doing most of the work in a group project.

_____
_____
_____
_____
_____
_____
_____
_____
_____
_____
_____
_____
_____
_____

5. Scenario: You are being ignored in a group conversation.

_____

_____

_____

_____

_____

_____

_____

_____

_____

_____

Activity 27: My School-Life Balance

A happy and healthy life involves striking a balance between school, home duties, and fun activities. When you put too much focus on one area, the other aspects of your life will suffer. Sure, making time for school is essential, but so is making time for playing video games, going outside, completing your house chores, being bored, and going out with friends.

To assess whether you have struck a good balance and are taking care of all your needs, complete the following instructions:

1. Choose and curate a list of six important life categories. For example, consider categories such as school, home duties, family, friends, health, hobbies, sports, relaxation, and pursuing your goals.
2. Under each category, write down the activities you do on a daily or weekly basis to address those needs. For example, under family, you might write:

   - helping my sibling with their homework
   - watching TV shows with my parents and siblings
   - helping my mom prepare dinner or set the table
   - playing video games with my dad

1. After you have written down the activities, identify categories that are empty, low, or overloaded with activities. Ask yourself why you spend so little or so much time on specific categories.
2. Think of ways to create more of a balance where each category is given a similar amount of time and importance in your life. For example, if there are too many serious activities in your weekly routine, add a few fun activities to allow yourself time to let loose and enjoy yourself. If you notice that you haven't prioritized certain categories like your health and goals, commit to at least two actions that you can take to improve those areas of your life.

Activity 28: Celebrating Personal Achievements

Setting meaningful goals is super important, but celebrating your wins along the way is just as crucial. You don't have to wait until you achieve your big goal to reward yourself; even small progress deserves recognition. Acknowledging these little victories boosts your confidence and keeps you motivated to keep going.

For this activity, think about something awesome you have done recently that has made you proud. It could be helping a classmate, learning a new skill, or completing a tough homework assignment. Follow the steps below to plan how you're going to celebrate it:

1. How much effort did you put into achieving this task? What obstacles did you overcome along the way?

_____

_____

_____

_____

_____

_____

_____

_____

_____

_____

_____

2. In what small way can you show yourself appreciation for making these improvements? It could be treating yourself to ice cream, going to the cinema with a friend, or preparing your favorite meal.

_____

_____

_____

_____

_____

_____

_____

3. Decide on when and how you will celebrate. It's important to be specific so that you are prepared for the event. For example, you might decide, "On Saturday afternoon, I will host a movie night sleepover with two of my friends to celebrate passing my test." Make sure you run your celebratory plans with your parents and anyone else you will need support from.

_____

_____

_____

_____

_____

_____

_____

_____

_____

_____

4. If your plans change and you aren't able to celebrate your achievement, reschedule to another date and time, but don't skip it! You deserve this moment of joy.

Activity 29: Goal Review and Reflection

At the start of this chapter, you set SMART goals in Activities 4 and 5. Now that a few weeks have gone by, it's time to check in on how you're doing with those goals and make any adjustments if needed. Use these questions to guide your reflection:

1. How much progress have I made toward my goals?

_____

_____

_____

_____

_____

_____

_____

2. What steps have worked well so far?

_____

_____

_____

_____

_____

_____

_____

_____

_____

_____

_____

_____

3. What challenges have I faced?

_____

_____

_____

_____

_____

_____

_____

_____

4. Do my goals still seem realistic and achievable?

_____

_____

_____

_____

_____

_____

_____

_____

_____

_____

_____

_____

5. What can I do differently to stay on track?

_____

_____

_____

_____

_____

_____

_____

_____

_____

_____

_____

_____

_____

_____

_____

_____

_____

Take a moment to think about your answers and
use them to tweak your goals if necessary.

Activity 30: Class Reflection and Sharing

Over the past 30 weeks, you've gotten a better handle on self-awareness and how it can boost your self-confidence. As a class, reflect on the activities you have done-what you enjoyed and what you found challenging. Share some cool new things you have discovered about yourself since you started these activities.

Think back to two moments during these 30 weeks: one where you felt really self-aware and one where you felt not so self-aware. What did you learn from both of those experiences? Listen to each other and see what you can learn from everyone's stories.

Being self-aware means knowing who you are inside out. This level of self-knowledge enables you to go through life with more confidence in your abilities and take action on the areas that need improvement. Continue to practice these SEL-based self-awareness activities to enhance your skills.

Strengths and Weaknesses Map

Use the blank page below to draw your strengths and weaknesses map based on the guidelines offered in Activity 2.

Drawing the Best Version of Me

Use the blank page below to draw a portrait of yourself based on the guidelines offered in Activity 7.

Accomplishment Timeline

Use the blank page below to draw a timeline of your accomplishments from elementary to middle school based on the guidelines offered in Activity 13.

Mind Mapping Interests and Hobbies

Use the blank page below, make a mind map of your interests and hobbies based on the guidelines offered in Activity 17.

Dear Future Me

Use the blank lines below to write a letter addressed to your future self based on the guidelines offered in Activity 20.

_____

_____

_____

_____

_____

_____

_____

_____

_____

_____

_____

_____

_____

_____

_____

_____

_____

_____

_____

_____

_____

_____

My Circle of Control

Write down the things within (inside the circle)
and outside of your control (outside of the circle)
based on the guidelines offered in Activity 24.

Answers (DO NOT LOOK AT THE ANSWERS UNTIL YOU HAVE COMPLETED THE CROSSWORD PUZZLE)

1. perseverance
2. challenge
3. mistakes
4. mindset
5. resilience
6. feedback
7. effort
8. growth
9. learning
10. persistence

Chapter - 2

Seventh Grade-Enhancing Social Skills and Self-Management

Nobody cares how much you know, until they know how much you care.

- Theodore Roosevelt

What Are Social Skills and Self-Management?

Social skills are the everyday behaviors used to communicate and build positive relationships. They involve expressing thoughts and feelings, listening, and validating others. Strong social skills help you thrive in various social situations, confidently share opinions, handle conflicts, and work well in teams. Self-management is about controlling your words and actions in different social contexts. It helps you avoid inappropriate behavior and makes others feel comfortable. On a personal level, it encourages thinking before acting, leading to positive outcomes for yourself and others.

Combining social skills and self-management improves your ability to handle any situation. You'll communicate openly and honestly, choose the right words, and avoid saying the wrong things. You'll also handle tough social situations better, like sharing ideas in a group, presenting in class, or resolving arguments with friends.

In this chapter, you'll explore scenarios like this and learn tools and strategies to handle them effectively.

 ## 30 Weeks of Fun: Social Skills and Self-Management Activities for Seventh-Grade Students

Do you ever feel shy when meeting new people, working in groups, or when asked to share your thoughts during class discussions? These types of social situations are common at school and impact how comfortable you feel in being yourself both in and out of the classroom. The following activities will help you build strong social skills and improve self-management so that you are prepared for any social situation that you might be faced with.

Activity 1: Mastering Clear Communication

Messages can get lost in translation, especially when communication isn't clear. Think of clear communication as explaining something to a little kid who doesn't know big words or complicated instructions. You need to keep it simple so that your ideas are easily understood.

For this activity, pair up with a classmate and sit back-to-back. One of you will get an object from the teacher, and the other will get paper and coloring pencils. The person with the object has to describe it in a way that's easy to understand so that the other person can draw it. The more specific and simpler your instructions, the better the drawing will turn out.

When you're done, turn around and compare the object with the drawing. See how well the description worked. If there's time, switch roles and try it again.

Activity 2: Yes, No, Maybe

Questions are super useful for understanding things better and clearing up confusion. This activity will help you learn the difference between closed and open questions. Closed questions only need a yes, no, or maybe answer, while open questions need more thought and detailed responses. The quality of feedback you get from your peers depends on the questions you ask them.

Split into two large groups with your classmates. Each group picks one person to go outside for 5 minutes to think of and write down the name of a classroom item on a piece of paper. When they come back, the rest of the group has to guess what the item is by asking 10 closed and open questions. If you can't guess it by the 10th question, the person reveals the answer. Then, it's someone else's turn to go outside and start the game again. As you play the game, notice the quality of information you get whenever you switch between closed and open questions.

Activity 3: Reading Your Body

Communication isn't always verbal. Some messages are conveyed through body language, like facial expressions, posture, and gestures. To become an effective communicator, you must learn how to interpret nonverbal messages and respond to them accordingly.

Reading Your Body is a fun activity that you can play in groups of 4-5. Each group will be given a list of nonverbal cues. One person will be chosen from the group to act out a particular cue and the rest of the group members need to guess what cue it is and what it means about the person. For example, if the cue is folding arms, the person could be feeling misunderstood, uncomfortable, or frustrated. Use this list of nonverbal cues to help you:

- *raising your eyebrows*
- *frowning*
- *scratching your head*
- *crossing your arms*
- *walking back and forth*
- *appearing distracted*
- *avoiding eye contact*
- *nodding your head*
- *moving away from someone*
- *rolling your eyes*

 ## Activity 4: The Compliment Sandwich

Constructive feedback helps someone improve by highlighting behaviors in a supportive and respectful manner. Though it can be hard to hear, when done right, it helps friends and classmates do better. One effective technique is the Compliment Sandwich. Start with something positive, mention what needs improvement, and end with another positive comment. This approach makes feedback easier to accept and shows you care.

Pair up and brainstorm ideas for a new tech gadget that could change everyday tasks. Each of you will come up with an idea separately, and then present your ideas to each other. While one presents, the other listens and takes notes on what they liked and what could be improved. After the presentation, use the Compliment Sandwich to give feedback.

For example: "I love how your gadget uses AI to assist with tasks (positive). One thing to improve might be making it different from ChatGPT, as it seems very similar right now (constructive). Overall, you explained the purpose well and your sketch is awesome (positive)."

After both presentations, exchange notes to review the feedback and improve your ideas. This exercise helps you learn how to give and receive feedback positively and effectively!

 Activity 5: Feedback Reflection Chart

After you have received constructive feedback from a teacher or classmate, take some time to process what they said or wrote down, and create a Feedback Reflection Chart by drawing a similar table to the one below:

Feedback Received	Tuesday	Wednesday	Thursday

- **Feedback Received:** Write down the exact comments you received from a teacher or classmate using their exact words.
- **Initial Reaction:** Note your immediate emotions when you got the feedback. Be honest, even if the reaction was unexpected.
- **Action Plan:** List three small steps you can take right now to implement the feedback. Focus on what you can change, like your habits, attitudes, or work process.
- **Results:** Write down the outcome after taking those steps. Reflect on how your skills, behavior, or process has improved. Allow at least three weeks for the new changes to take effect before you assess the results.

Activity 6: Walk in Their Shoes

When interacting with different people, you learn that not everyone shares the same thoughts and feelings. Age, confidence levels, and cultural backgrounds can lead to diverse perspectives and expressions. In this activity, you'll "walk in someone else's shoes" to understand their thoughts and feelings. Walking in someone else's shoes teaches you the value of appreciating others' unique perspectives.

Below are scenario cards with characters facing specific challenges. Read their stories and reflect on what you would do in their situation. Consider questions like:

- How does the person feel in their situation?
- What challenges are they facing?
- How do these challenges impact their behavior?
- What type of support does this person need?
- How can classmates or friends make the person feel included?

Scenario cards

Scenario: You are a new student who has just moved to this town and who will be starting at this school today. You don't know anyone, and you feel nervous and overwhelmed.
Reflection: Consider how it feels to be in an unfamiliar environment without any friends. What kind of welcome would make you feel more comfortable? How can your classmates help you feel included?
Scenario: You are a student who has recently moved from another country. Your customs, language, and way of life are different from those of your classmates. Sometimes, they don't understand you, and you feel left out.
Reflection: Think about the challenges of adapting to a new culture and language. How would you want others to treat you? What can classmates do to make you feel more accepted and understood?

Scenario: You are a student with a physical disability that requires you to use a wheelchair. Some parts of the school are difficult to navigate, and you sometimes feel isolated because of your mobility challenges.

Reflection: Reflect on the physical and emotional challenges you might face. How would you feel if your peers ignored or underestimated you? What actions can others take to be more inclusive and supportive?

Scenario: You are a teacher who is passionate about helping students learn, but you notice that some students are disengaged and disruptive in class. You're trying to find ways to make your lessons more engaging.

Reflection: Consider the pressures and responsibilities of being a teacher. How would you feel if your efforts to teach were met with disinterest or disrespect? What can students do to show appreciation and make the classroom a better environment for learning?

Scenario: You are the school janitor who works hard to keep the school clean and safe for everyone. Sometimes, students make messes and don't seem to care about the work you do.

Reflection: Think about the pride and effort you put into your work. How would it feel to have your efforts go unnoticed or disrespected? What can students do to show respect and appreciation for the custodial staff?

 ## Activity 7: Agree to Disagree

It's okay to have a difference of opinion when having conversations with your friends and classmates. What matters is not that you disagree, but rather how you express your disagreement to others, and that you swiftly move the conversation along without hurting feelings.

Get into pairs and act out of a scenario below where two people might reach a disagreement. Use the disagreement scripts provided to practice expressing your opinions while showing kindness and keeping the conversation going.

Scenarios

1. Favorite sports teams
Person A: Thinks soccer is the best sport.
Person B: Believes basketball is superior.

2. Movie preferences

Person A: Loves action movies.
Person B: Prefers romantic comedies.

3. School subjects

Person A: Thinks math is the most important subject.
Person B: Believes literature is more valuable.

4. Vacation destinations

Person A: Wants to go to the beach.
Person B: Prefers the mountains.

Disagreement Scripts

- *"I understand your point and see why you feel that way, but..."*
- *"That's an interesting viewpoint. Personally, I think..."*
- *"I believe that because..."*
- *"From my experience, I've found that..."*
- *"My perspective is based on..."*
- *"Even though we have different views, it's great that we can discuss this."*
- *"It's cool that we both care about this topic, even if we see it differently."*
- *"I respect your opinion, even though I don't share it."*
- *"Since we both care about this topic, what do you think about...?"*
- *"Let's talk about something we both enjoy, like..."*

Activity 8: Thriving as a Team

Teamwork can be tough if you aim to outshine others or let them do all the work. Instead, recognize that everyone brings unique strengths and abilities, including you. Sharing these with your team helps everyone learn and contribute positively to the project.

With this mindset, form groups of 4-5 and get ready for an exciting business project. Your teacher will give you random materials to create a product to sell at local stores. To succeed, brainstorm ideas, embrace different perspectives, and use the "Thriving as a Team" page for brainstorming.

Practice giving constructive feedback and expressing disagreements kindly *(refer to Activities 4 and 7 for help)*. Decide as a group how to present your product to the class, whether by dressing up, creating a poster, or making a short advert for social media. Think big and creatively to maximize the strengths and abilities of all your team members.

Activity 9: Team Roles and Contributions

Successful teams are well-organized, with each member assigned clear duties to achieve project goals. For this activity, form groups of 4-5 and build a DIY solar oven to cook a small snack using the sun's power.

Assign the following roles based on strengths:
- **Project Manager:** Oversees the project, tracks time, keeps the team focused, and coordinates efforts.
- **Materials Coordinator:** Manages materials, ensures all supplies are ready, and organizes storage.
- **Design Specialist:** Plans and designs the solar oven, ensuring functionality.
- **Construction Expert:** Leads the building process, follows design plans, and assembles the oven.
- **Quality Checker:** Inspects the work, tests the oven, and makes necessary adjustments.

Once roles are assigned, follow the steps to create your DIY solar oven and make sun s'mores.

Materials
- 1 large cardboard box (pizza box works great)
- Aluminum foil
- Black construction paper
- Clear plastic wrap
- Glue, tape, and scissors
- Rulers and markers

Instructions
1. Lay a large cardboard box flat on the ground.
2. Using a ruler and marker, draw a square on the top of the box, 2 inches from the edges.
3. Create a flap by cutting across three sides of the square. Leave one side untouched so you can open and close the top of the box. With a pair of scissors, neatly cut out a flap.
4. Cut a piece of aluminum foil roughly the size of the flap, glue it to the inside of the flap, and smooth it out to reflect sunlight.
5. Cut a piece of black construction paper the same size as the flat surface inside the box, glue it down, and press firmly. This absorbs heat to aid cooking.
6. Seal all edges and holes of the box with tape to trap heat.
7. Place a small piece of aluminum foil on the black paper inside the box to reflect more sunlight and act as a tray.
8. Put a small snack (like cheese or a marshmallow) on the foil tray.
9. Position the oven in a sunny spot outside, angle the flap to maximize sunlight, and let it sit for 30-60 minutes, depending on sunlight and snack type.

10. Check the snack periodically, and when it's cooked to your liking, carefully remove it and enjoy!

After you have completed the project, sit together with your team and reflect on the following questions:
- *What went well in the project?*
- *Were there any challenges? If so, how did you overcome them?*
- *How did each person's role contribute to the success of the project?*
- *What would you do differently next time?*

 ## Activity 10: Solving a Classroom Dilemma

Problem-solving is a key social skill that helps address challenges affecting you and others. Group problem-solving is often more effective than working alone. In this activity, you'll work in small groups to solve one of the classroom dilemmas provided. You'll also explore problem-solving techniques to address the issue effectively.

Use the blank page at the end of the chapter titled "Solving a Classroom Dilemma" for brainstorming. At the end, present your solution to the class and explain which problem-solving techniques you used.

Classroom Dilemmas (Choose One)
1. **Scenario 1:** *During a group project, Alex and Jordan disagree on the project's direction–Alex wants a detailed report, while Jordan prefers a multimedia presentation. This disagreement is causing frustration and delays.*
2. **Scenario 2:** *Several students consistently miss homework deadlines, forcing the teacher to spend extra time with them and disrupting the learning experience for everyone.*
3. **Scenario 3:** *Some students are disruptive during lessons, making it hard for others to focus. Despite the teacher's efforts, the issue persists.*

Problem-Solving Techniques (Choose Any)
- **Root cause analysis:** *Define the problem, use a cause-and-effect diagram to identify potential causes, and develop solutions addressing these root causes.*
- **The five whys:** *State the problem, ask "why" repeatedly until you identify the root cause, and brainstorm solutions that target it directly.*
- **Pros and cons list:** *List the benefits and drawbacks of each potential solution, then compare them to choose the most advantageous option.*
- **Decision matrix:** *Create a table listing potential solutions and important criteria (e.g., cost, effectiveness), rate each solution, and calculate scores to find the best one.*
- **Reverse brainstorming:** *Instead of solving the problem, identify ways to worsen it. Use these insights to determine what to avoid and how to address the actual problem effectively.*

Activity 11: Practice Being CALM

Some conversations with teachers or classmates might be tough, stirring up emotions like anger or disappointment. Using the CALM technique helps you regain control and think clearly about your choices. Here's how to practice it:

- **C: Check-in**

Before responding, take 30 seconds to breathe deeply and calm yourself. Ask, "What am I feeling right now?" Treat your feelings with the same compassion you would for a close friend.

- **A: Assess the Situation**

Once calm, evaluate what happened. Identify what actions or words affected you and ask, "Why did this make me emotional?"

- **L: Listen to the Other Person**

If confused, ask the other person to explain and listen carefully. Show you're listening by nodding and maintaining eye contact.

- **M: Mindful Response**

After understanding the situation and the other person's perspective, share your feelings using "I feel" statements and request a change. For example, "I feel anxious when you raise your voice. Could you lower your voice so that we can talk calmly?"

Pair up with a classmate to practice this technique by acting out scenarios where CALM can be used, like someone making fun of you or spilling a drink on your textbooks. Switch roles to experience both perspectives.

 ## Activity 12: Seek PEACE With Others

Sometimes, you might hurt someone's feelings. When that happens, seek PEACE to resolve the situation. PEACE is an acronym for the steps to take when you need to apologize. If you feel guilty but don't know what to say, follow these five steps to restore harmony:

- **P: Pause**-Reflect on the situation before approaching the other person. Consider how it unfolded, what actions were taken, and the outcome.

- **E: Empathize**-Put yourself in the other person's shoes. Understand their feelings and how your actions affected them.

- **A: Apologize**–Apologize specifically for what you regret. Acknowledge their feelings with phrases like "I know I disappointed you."

- **C: Commit**–Promise to improve your behavior. Offer a specific action you will take to avoid repeating the mistake.

- **E: Exchange positive words**–End on a positive note by expressing something kind about the other person, such as appreciating their courage.

For this activity, pair up with a classmate to role-play a scenario where someone needs to make amends. Practice the PEACE steps, then switch roles to apply the technique effectively.

 ## Activity 13: Mediation Training

When you need to mediate a conflict between friends or classmates, your role is to be neutral and help both sides understand each other's viewpoints. Mediation is like problem-solving and involves these steps:

1. *Ensure everyone feels respected by agreeing on rules like "no yelling or interrupting."*
2. *Allow each person 5 minutes to share their side of the story. Take notes on key issues and needs, like trust or honesty.*
3. *Offer constructive feedback and suggest ways to resolve the issues. Give each person 5 minutes to respond to your suggestions.*
4. *Write down the final agreement. If no consensus is reached, encourage respect for each other's differences and peaceful resolution.*

In groups of three, role-play a dispute with a mediator (a friend, teacher, or parent). Switch roles to ensure everyone gets a chance to mediate, using the steps above while adding your own style to make it engaging.

Activity 14: Profiling Young Activists

If you want to polish your social skills, you can study the speaking styles and techniques used by famous young activists like Greta Thunberg, Malala Yousafzai, and Jaylen Arnold. What's similar about these young people is their confidence in standing up for what they believe in, even when it goes against the norm.

For this activity, pick a young activist under 30 who has awesome communication skills. Do some background research on them to learn how they started their activism journey. Identify at least five speaking techniques they use in their speeches and interviews to make their message clear and inspire change. Finally, prepare a speech about the activist you chose, and while giving your speech, try to use the same techniques they do.

 ## Activity 15: Time Detective

We often go through the day without thinking about how we are using our time. Before we know it, the day is over, but there are still tasks waiting to be completed. Time Detective is a fun activity that will help you keep track of your time throughout the day so that you can know where it is being spent and how to use it more effectively. This activity is supposed to continue for a full week, so commit to tracking your time every day.

Here's what you need to do:

- *Write down five tasks that you need to get done before the day is over. Your list might include things like eating breakfast, going to school, doing homework, completing house chores, and watching an episode of your favorite show.*

- *Use a stopwatch to time yourself completing each task. For longer tasks like "going to school" that take several hours to complete, simply record the normal times your school starts and ends.*

- *Continue to track your time until the end of the week, then total the number of hours you spent on each task-notice where most of your time is being spent and the type of tasks you have prioritized.*

- *Bring your table and findings to class and share the insights you learned in a small group. Help each other find ways of managing time more effectively.*

Table Example:

	Monday	Tuesday	Wednesday	Thursday	Friday
Early morning workout	15 minutes	20 minutes	15 minutes	10 minutes	15 minutes
Go to school	8 hours	8 hours	8 hours	8 hours	8 hours
Homework and study sessions	1 hour	30 minutes	30 minutes	1.5 hours	15 minutes
Free time	3 hours	5 hours	3.5 hours	5 hours	5 hours
Browsing social media	3 hours	2.5 hours	2.5 hours	3 hours	4 hours

	End of week total
Early morning workout	1 hour 15 minutes
Going to school	40 hours
Homework and study sessions	3 hours 45 minutes
Free time	21 hours 30 minutes
Browsing social media	15 hours

Note that not everybody will have the same tasks carried out five days a week. Some tasks could be performed on certain days and not others. Just make sure that all tasks are recorded and totaled.

Activity 16: Task Prioritization

After you have reflected on where your time is being spent, the next step is to distinguish between urgent, important, and unimportant tasks. Using the time tracking tables that you created in the previous activity, sort your tasks into four categories:

- **Urgent and important:** *You need to get these tasks done immediately or you may face negative consequences!*
- **Important but not urgent:** *These tasks are related to your goals and add value to your life. Get them done as soon as you can so that you can feel good about yourself.*
- **Appears urgent but not important:** *These sneaky tasks make themselves seem bigger and more urgent than they are. Your day wouldn't be negatively impacted if you rescheduled them.*
- **Not urgent and not important:** *Tasks that are big time wasters and distractions fall under this category. They are unproductive and leave you feeling regretful for wasting so much time.*

Based on the example given above, here is how the tasks would be sorted:

Urgent and important	• Going to school • Homework and study sessions
Important but not urgent	• Early morning workout
Appears urgent but not important	• Free time
Not urgent and not important	• Browsing social media

Activity 17: Self-Care Prioritization

Were you aware that your self-care is a priority task that needs to be incorporated into your daily routine? Self-care means nourishing your mind and body through healthy activities like eating a balanced diet, getting enough sleep, exercising, treating yourself to a snack, journaling, taking a nap, or seeking support if you need it. These activities manage your stress levels and moods, ensuring that you enjoy each day.

For this activity, you are required to answer some questions that can help you reflect on how much you prioritize self-care and can help you look for ways to show more commitment.

Physical Self-Care

How often do you participate in physical activities that get your heart rate up? Do you think it's enough to maintain a healthy lifestyle?

_____

_____

_____

_____

_____

_____

_____

_____

_____

_____

_____

_____

_____

_____

_____

_____

_____

_____

_____

During times when you are active, do you notice changes to your mood and energy levels? If so, what are some of those changes?

_____

_____

_____

_____

_____

_____

_____

_____

Are there any physical activities that you enjoy but haven't done in a while? If so, what has been holding you back?

_____

_____

_____

_____

_____

_____

_____

_____

_____

_____

Mental and Emotional Self-Care

Do you have hobbies that stimulate your mind? If so, how much time do you spend on them?

_____

_____

_____

_____

_____

_____

_____

_____

_____

_____

_____

_____

_____

_____

_____

_____

_____

_____

_____

_____

_____

_____

_____

What are your go-to strategies for managing stress and anxiety? How often do you practice these strategies?

_____

_____

_____

_____

_____

_____

_____

_____

_____

When you are feeling down, who do you typically reach out to for a chat? Who else within your circle of friends and family can offer support?

_____

_____

_____

_____

_____

_____

_____

_____

_____

_____

_____

Social Self-Care

Do you make time to spend with your family and friends? Are you satisfied with the amount of interactions you currently have with your family and friends?

_____

_____

_____

_____

_____

_____

_____

_____

_____

_____

_____

_____

_____

_____

_____

_____

_____

_____

_____

_____

_____

_____

What would make you more enthusiastic about spending time with your family and friends? For instance, are there certain activities you can do together or certain habits you can adopt?

_____

_____

_____

_____

_____

_____

_____

Can you identify a relationship that you value but haven't put effort into maintaining? What small action can you take to start investing more effort into this relationship?

_____

_____

_____

_____

_____

_____

_____

_____

_____

_____

How often do you explore social outdoor activities like going to the cinema, window shopping, meeting up with friends, or connecting with a social club? What obstacles have gotten in the way?

_____

_____

_____

_____

_____

_____

_____

_____

_____

What new social activities are you willing to try at least once in the next three months? These can be solo or group activities. Write them down and set goals that you can commit to.

_____

_____

_____

_____

_____

_____

_____

_____

_____

_____

_____

_____

Activity 18: Finding My Self-Care Buddy

Even though self-care practices are important, the truth is that performing them consistently requires ongoing motivation, which you may not always display. To help you commit to your self-care practices, find yourself a self-care buddy who enjoys the same activities and needs encouragement too.

The purpose of this activity is to match you with a classmate so you can support each other in staying healthy. The first thing to do is to fill out the Self-Care Buddy Questionnaire, which can be found at the end of the chapter. Thereafter, tear out the page and submit your filled-out questionnaire to your teacher, who will go through all of the results and match students based on their self-care interests.

Once you have been matched with your self-care buddy, arrange a date where you can meet to establish self-care goals, create a self-care schedule, and discuss how often you will check in with each other's progress during the week.

 ## Activity 19: Assessing My Academic Needs

The higher your grade level, the more academic demands are placed on you. Keeping up with these expectations can be tough, especially when you are dealing with a few academic challenges and need additional help. By assessing your academic needs, you can identify the gaps in your skills and knowledge and proactively seek the guidance and support you need.

Answer the following questions as honestly as you can to assess your academic needs and performance.

1. What subjects do you find challenging?

_____

_____

_____

_____

_____

_____

_____

_____

_____

_____

2. For each subject mentioned, what specific topics or concepts do you have trouble understanding or practicing?

_____

_____

_____

_____

_____

_____

_____

_____

_____

_____

_____

_____

3. What are your thoughts about your current study habits and schedules? Do you allocate enough time for studying or making notes each week? Are you satisfied with your study methods?

_____

_____

_____

_____

_____

_____

_____

_____

4. How comfortable are you with seeking help and asking questions when you don't understand something? What thoughts, feelings, or obstacles get in your way?

_____

_____

_____

_____

_____

_____

_____

_____

_____

_____

5. Besides your teacher, what other resources do you use to find relevant information? For example, do you search online, visit the library, ask a friend, or attend a study group?

_____

_____

_____

_____

_____

_____

_____

_____

_____

6. Based on the answers provided for the previous questions, what seems to be the main challenges you are facing academically? Make a list of them.

_____

_____

_____

_____

_____

_____

_____

_____

_____

_____

_____

_____

7. For each academic challenge identified, list three resources that you can turn to for additional support. Try to mention different resources for each challenge.

_____

_____

_____

_____

_____

_____

_____

_____

_____

_____

7. Lastly, set boundaries for each challenge to help you determine when it's time to set up a meeting with your parents and teachers to discuss more structured support like enrolling in special education services. Start your boundaries with the following phrase: *When [name a specific outcome] happens, then I will know I need to involve my parents and teachers.* **For example, "When I cannot seem to focus in class despite moving seats and paying attention to the teacher, then I'll know that I will need to involve my parents and teachers."**

_____

_____

_____

_____

_____

_____

_____

_____

_____

Activity 20: Trust Self-Assessment

Trust is the building block of healthy relationships with friends, classmates, and teachers. Your level of trust with others depends on your willingness to open up and share aspects of who you are with other people. Take the Trust Self-Assessment, which you can find at the end of the chapter. Afterward, reflect on your responses and consider the opportunities for increasing your trust levels and strengthening your connections with others.

 ## Activity 21: Building Trust Through Open Dialogue

With the awareness of your trust levels, challenge yourself to begin opening up to others more. Think of this as your way of practicing sharing your stories and actively listening to others. Get into pairs with a classmate and go through the series of conversation prompts below, sharing information that you are comfortable with other people knowing about you.

After responding to the prompt, your classmate will ask you at least one follow-up question before moving on to the next prompt. When you have gone through all of the prompts, it's your classmate's turn to share. At the end of the activity, sit by yourself and reflect on what you found enjoyable and challenging about sharing these stories.

Prompts
- *Share one of your favorite childhood memories.*
- *Describe a time in your life when you hated school.*
- *Mention an activity that is on your hobbies bucket list.*
- *Talk about your dream career or work environment.*
- *Talk about your plans for life after high school.*
- *Describe a personal achievement that makes you proud.*
- *Open up about a fear that you have that other people find silly or strange.*
- *Mention a core value or belief that is meaningful for you and guides your actions.*

 ## Activity 22: Fireside Storytelling

Back in the day, before we had all our tech gadgets, families would gather around the fireplace to share stories. This was a great way to keep everyone, young and old, connected and entertained. You can create that same sense of connection with your classmates by playing a game called *Fireside Storytelling*.

Find a cool legend or folktale from your culture and write it down. Seek to understand what the story reveals about your culture's beliefs and traditions, and then get ready to share it with your class.

On presentation day, arrange yourselves in a circle and imagine that there's a cozy fire in the middle. Take turns sharing your stories with the group. As everyone presents, take a moment to appreciate the diverse ideas, values, and traditions that each person brings to the circle.

 ## Activity 23: Blindfolded Food Tasting

Here is another activity that can help you strengthen trust with your classmates. It's called *Blindfolded Food Tasting*. As the name suggests, you are required to eat a range of snacks while blindfolded and guess what they are. Prepare your tastebuds for sweet, sour, savory, and spicy delicacies.

Here's how it works:
1. *Team up with a classmate. Each of you will bring six snacks.*
2. *Pack your snacks in small, sealable plastic bags or containers-no need for big packets.*
3. *Blindfold your partner, and then let them taste each snack one by one.*
4. *Your partner will try to guess what each snack is, relying on their taste buds and your guidance.*
5. *Switch places and have them blindfold you so you can complete a taste test too.*

The goal is to trust that your partner will choose snacks that are fun and perhaps weird, but not something unpleasant, making the experience enjoyable for both of you.

 ## Activity 24: Talking About Embarrassing Moments

We all have embarrassing moments that make us want to bury our heads in the sand or hide behind a tree. However, instead of feeling bad about these moments, we can speak about them to practice accepting our imperfections and not be so tough on ourselves.

For this activity, you are required to write about an embarrassing experience on paper, fold it in half, and place it inside a bowl. Sit in a circle with your classmates and pass the bowl around so that each person can pick a random piece of paper, read the note out loud, and empathize with what the person who wrote it went through. If the note is funny, you can laugh but show some kindness too by offering words of encouragement.

Finally, guess who wrote the note. If you fail after a few attempts, the students who wrote it must reveal themselves and briefly share the story of what happened and what they have learned from the situation.

Activity 25: Digital Citizenship Basics

How you conduct yourself online is just as important as how you conduct yourself in real life. There are some basic rules of etiquette that you need to remember when surfing the net, particularly when engaging with users.

To find out more about what these rules are, pretend that a family of aliens has just landed on Earth and needs guidelines on how to "act normal" on the internet so that people don't discover their real identities. Put together a manual of safe behaviors they need to follow when interacting with users online. You can organize the information into categories, such as how to behave on social media, forums, emails, messaging apps, and live-streaming platforms. Provide at least five detailed points for each category. You will need access to the internet so you can browse websites to complete this activity.

 ## Activity 26: Anti-Bullying Awareness

Online bullying (also called cyberbullying) is a serious form of emotional abuse that involves using technology to harass, intimidate, or make fun of targeted people. Examples of online bullying include:

- *sending rude text messages*
- *gossiping and spreading rumors about someone*
- *making threats to hurt someone or leak personal information*
- *sharing insensitive photos or videos designed to embarrass someone*
- *making nasty comments about someone's physical appearance or living situation*

Not only can online bullying shatter someone's self-esteem, it can also lead to anxiety, trust issues, depression, eating disorders, sleep problems, and other mental health issues.

In this activity, you are required to get into groups and design an anti-bullying awareness poster using information about online bullying that you have sourced online. The main part of your poster should be to introduce an acronym that provides young people with strategies on how to deal with online bullying when they are targeted or see it happening to someone else.

Activity 27: Managing Screen Time

It can be easy to lose track of how much time you spend on your electronic devices, whether you binge on Netflix series, play video games, or scroll through social media feeds. A great way to maintain a balance between online and offline activities to practice monitoring your screen usage.

One way to do this is to schedule time in your day for using devices and set daily limits. Be strict with yourself to only use your device within the time allocated. For example, if you have scheduled time to browse TikTok when you get home from school, do not open the app in the morning or during school hours. Wait until after school to get on the app.

Secondly, set specific time limits to avoid hours of scrolling. For example, you might decide that 2.5 hours a day is enough social media usage. You can split the time into 2 or 3 smaller sessions or enjoy one long session of browsing. When the time is up, close the app and find an offline activity to do like cleaning your room, reading a book, or taking a shower.

Below is an example of how you could schedule screen time into your daily routine. Use the example to update your current routine:

Times	Activities
6:30 a.m. to 7:30 a.m.	**Morning routine:** • Wake up, shower, get dressed, have breakfast. • No screen time.
7:30 a.m. to 4:00 p.m.	**School hours:** • Focus on school activities and classes. • No screen time (unless necessary for schoolwork).
4:00 p.m. to 5:00 p.m.	**Homework/study time:** • Finish homework and study for any upcoming tests. • Screen time: Allowed only if needed for schoolwork.

5:00 p.m. to 6:00 p.m.	**Outdoor activities/exercise:** • Engage in physical activities like playing sports, going for a walk, or exercising. • No screen time.
6:00 p.m. to 7:00 p.m.	**Dinner time:** • Have dinner with family. • No screen time.
7:00 p.m. to 9:00 p.m.	**Leisure time:** • Screen time: 2 hours (watching a TV show, playing video games, or browsing social media).
9:00 p.m.	**Prepare for bed:** • Night routine: brushing teeth, changing into pajamas, and relaxing before sleep. • No screen time.

Activity 28: Thank-You Notes

Some students and teachers make your school experience easier and more enjoyable. Show your appreciation to these people by writing them thank-you notes. Your message doesn't need to be long for it to be heartfelt. Focus on one or two things each individual has done to support you and express how much their words, actions, and company mean to you. If you enjoy this activity, turn it into a monthly practice where you identify someone to thank for being awesome!

Activity 29: Setting Communication Boundaries

Your friends and classmates won't automatically know what behaviors make you upset. Whenever your feelings are hurt during conversations, take the opportunity to set communication boundaries and tell them what you need. The DESO technique is a smart way of structuring your message to ensure that your boundaries are clearly communicated.

Here's how you can follow the DESO technique:

- *D: Describe*–Describe the upsetting behavior you noticed. Focus on the actions of the person and not their character.
- *E: Express*–Share the emotional impact of the behavior, such as how you felt at the moment and afterward. Use the "I felt [emotion] when...." statement.
- *S: Specify*–Be specific about the desired behavior you would like to see moving forward. Now is your time to set a boundary.
- *O: Outcome*–Mention what you foresee happening if the person's behavior doesn't change. For instance, what actions will you be forced to take?

Example

Scenario: Your friend shares a secret that you told them not to tell anybody.

- *D:* "I noticed that you shared the news meant to be kept secret between us."
- *E:* "I felt angry and betrayed when I saw that because I trusted you."
- *S:* "Moving forward, I need you to ask for my permission before sharing my personal information."
- *O:* "If the same thing happens again, I won't be able to confide in you anymore."

Practice going through the DESO technique using the following scenarios:

- **Scenario 1:** A classmate keeps interrupting you when you're speaking during group discussions.

_____

_____

_____

_____

_____

_____

_____

_____

_____

_____

_____

Scenario 2: *A friend makes jokes about something you're sensitive about in front of others.*

_____

_____

_____

_____

_____

_____

_____

_____

_____

_____

- **Scenario 3:** *A teammate doesn't contribute equally to a group project, leaving you with most of the work.*

_____

_____

_____

_____

_____

_____

_____

_____

_____

_____

_____

_____

_____

Activity 30: Value-Friendship Alignment

Friendships make up a core component of your social life. They shape your attitudes, behaviors, and memories of childhood. To ensure that you have positive and supportive friends around you, you need to assess whether they promote and protect the things that you value. If they don't, you will need to learn how to express your needs so that your friends can change their behaviors and make you feel respected and comfortable.

Go through the following questions to reflect on your values and friendships:

1. What are the most important qualities that make someone a friend?

_____

_____

_____

_____

_____

_____

_____

_____

_____

_____

_____

_____

_____

_____

_____

_____

2. What does friendship support look like for you?

_____

_____

_____

_____

_____

_____

_____

_____

3. What type of phrases do you like hearing from a friend?

_____

_____

_____

_____

_____

_____

_____

_____

_____

_____

_____

_____

4. What are the signs that someone isn't your friend?

_____

_____

_____

_____

_____

_____

_____

_____

5. Think about a person whom you consider a friend. What qualities do they display that you value?

_____

_____

_____

_____

_____

_____

_____

_____

_____

_____

_____

_____

6. How do you often feel after spending time with this friend?

_____

_____

_____

_____

_____

_____

_____

_____

_____

7. How do they show support? Is it in the way that you prefer friends to support you?

_____

_____

_____

_____

_____

_____

_____

_____

_____

_____

_____

_____

8. Does your friend have any qualities or behaviors that you find unkind or disrespectful?

_____

_____

_____

_____

_____

_____

_____

_____

_____

_____

If there are certain behaviors that your friend displays that don't align with your values, it's important to speak up and express your needs. Use the following needs statement to make your requests known:

"I really value [core value (e.g., honesty)] in my friendships. It's important to me because [reason]. I feel [emotion] when [specific behavior]. I would appreciate it if we could [suggest change or action] to make our friendship stronger."

_____

_____

_____

_____

_____

_____

_____

_____

Mastering social skills and self-management allows you to express your genuine thoughts and feelings without hurting others. In this way, you can improve the quality of your relationships and learn to solve social problems effectively. Practice the activities mentioned in this chapter regularly to feel confident in any social situation you encounter, whether inside or outside of the classroom!

Thriving as a Team

Use the blank page below to brainstorm your creative product based on the guidelines offered in Activity 8.

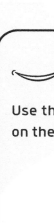

Solving a Classroom Dilemma

Use the blank page below to brainstorm your creative solution for solving a classroom dilemma based on the guidelines offered in Activity 10.

Self-Care Buddy Questionnaire

Fill out the questionnaire below to explore your self-care interests. Afterward, submit the questionnaire to your teacher, who will help you find a compatible self-care buddy.

Name: _____

Grade: _____

Favorite Self-Care Activities

Which of the following self-care activities do you enjoy? (Check all that apply)
- *Reading*
- *Writing/journaling*
- *Drawing/painting*
- *Playing sports/exercising*
- *Meditating*
- *Listening to music*
- *Cooking/baking*
- *Watching movies/TV shows*
- *Playing an instrument*
- *Gardening*
- *Doing puzzles/brain games*
- *Practicing yoga*
- *Spending time outdoors*
- *Talking with friends/family*
- *Other (please specify):* _____

How often do you practice self-care activities?
- *Daily*
- *Several times a week*
- *Once a week*
- *Occasionally*

What time of day do you usually prefer for self-care activities?
- *Morning*
- *Afternoon*
- *Evening*

What self-care activity helps you feel the most relaxed and happy?
(Please describe in a few sentences)

_____

_____

_____

_____

_____

_____

_____

_____

_____

_____

Are you interested in trying new self-care activities with a buddy?

- Yes
- No

Do you prefer self-care activities that are quiet and calm, or active and energetic?

- Quiet and calm
- Active and energetic
- Both

Is there anything specific you look for in a self-care buddy?

(e.g., similar hobbies, someone who motivates you, etc.)

_____

_____

_____

_____

_____

_____

_____

_____

_____

Thank you for completing the survey!

For Teacher Only

Student 1 Name:

Student 2 Name:

Shared Activities:

_____

_____

_____

_____

_____

_____

_____

_____

_____

_____

_____

Additional Notes:

_____

_____

_____

_____

_____

_____

_____

Trust Self-Assessment

Take the trust self-assessment below, and then reflect on your ability to trust yourself and others and possible areas of improvements.

Questionnaire

Instructions:
For each statement below, rate how much you agree or disagree using the following scale:
1. -Strongly Disagree
2. -Disagree
3. -Neutral
4. -Agree
5. -Strongly Agree

Remember to be honest with yourself so you can use these responses as constructive feedback to improve your relationships.

Trust Self-Assessment Statements:
I feel comfortable sharing my ideas with my classmates.
- 1 2 3 4 5

I trust my classmates to keep their promises.
- 1 2 3 4 5

I believe my classmates have good intentions toward me.
- 1 2 3 4 5

I am open to receiving feedback from my classmates.
- 1 2 3 4 5

I feel confident asking for help from my classmates when needed.
- 1 2 3 4 5

I am comfortable sharing personal information with my classmates.
- 1 2 3 4 5

I believe my classmates will support me during difficult times.
- 1 2 3 4 5

I trust my classmates to respect my opinions and ideas.
- 1 2 3 4 5

I am willing to collaborate with my classmates on group projects.
- 1 2 3 4 5

I feel that my classmates value my contributions to discussions and activities.
- 1 2 3 4 5

Reflection Questions:

What patterns did you notice in your responses?

_____

_____

_____

_____

_____

_____

_____

_____

_____

Reflect on areas where you rated yourself high or low. What might these patterns indicate about your trust levels?

_____

_____

_____

_____

_____

_____

_____

_____

_____

_____

_____

_____

_____

Are there specific situations where you feel less trusting?

_____

_____

_____

_____

_____

_____

_____

_____

Consider any situations or contexts where your trust levels might be lower. What could be causing these feelings?

_____

_____

_____

_____

_____

_____

_____

_____

_____

_____

_____

_____

What steps can you take to improve trust in your relationships with classmates?

_____

_____

_____

_____

_____

_____

_____

_____

_____

_____

How can understanding your own trust levels help you build stronger relationships?

_____

_____

_____

_____

_____

_____

_____

_____

_____

_____

_____

_____

_____

Chapter - 3

Eighth Grade-Leadership and Future Planning

Don't ask what the world needs. Ask what makes you come alive, and go do it. Because what the world needs is people who have come alive.

- Howard Thurman

 What Is Leadership and Future Planning?

When you think of a leader, you might picture someone who's outgoing, smart, or popular. But being a leader is more about one's dedication to improving life for others and about taking responsibility for their actions. Leaders find creative solutions, solve problems, and enhance their communities, setting an example for positive change.

Leadership isn't limited to specific ages or titles. Leaders can be CEOs, team captains, debate club heads, or even young volunteers in your community. It's not about inventing something new but making existing ideas work better, cheaper, or more sustainably.

Future planning isn't just for adults; it starts in middle school and continues throughout life. It involves setting short-term and long-term goals and figuring out how to achieve them.

For example, you might plan your transition from middle to high school and later decide on college, a gap year, volunteering, or entering the workforce. Planning ahead helps reduce stress and makes you feel more prepared for the future.

Developing leadership and future planning skills boosts your confidence and independence. They help you understand yourself better, solve problems creatively, and make decisions that positively impact your life and others. Future planning helps you set ambitious goals and work towards them, looking two to five years ahead at all times.

Consider Malala Yousafzai, the youngest Nobel Peace Prize winner. At just 11, she started a blog about girls' education challenges under Taliban rule. Despite threats, she continued advocating for education, eventually creating the Malala Fund to help girls from disadvantaged communities (ElevatEd, 2021). Her story exemplifies leadership through problem-solving, accountability, and decision-making and future planning through vision and goal-setting.

In this chapter, you will learn to develop these skills to make a positive impact on your life and community!

 30 Weeks of Fun: Leadership and Future Planning Activities for Eighth-Grade Students

To make a positive impact in the world, you need to develop a strong belief in yourself and be willing to follow the path of your passions and dreams. The following activities provide creative ways to learn more about your values, interests, and passions.

 Activity 1: Quiz-What's Your Leadership Style?

Have you ever sat down and wondered what type of leader you would be? Maybe you are the type who loves asking others for their opinions and feedback so they can assist in the decision-making process. Or maybe you are the type of leader who is comfortable taking charge and making decisions on their own. In this quiz, you will discover your the leadership style that suits your personality.

Read through the following statements and circle the letter that describes how you would normally handle each scenario. When you are done, tally up your scores for each letter and see your results.

1. When organizing a group project, you prefer that
- *A) everyone shares their ideas, and you decide together on the best approach.*
- *B) you make the final decision on how the project will be done and assign tasks.*
- *C) you inspire the group with your vision and motivate everyone to contribute towards achieving it.*

2. If there's a disagreement in your group, you
- A) facilitate a discussion to find a compromise that everyone agrees on.
- B) decide on the solution yourself and instruct the group on the next steps.
- C) encourage the group to focus on the ultimate goal and how resolving the conflict aligns with it.

3. When setting goals for a group project, you
- A) set goals collaboratively with input from everyone to ensure they're achievable and motivating for the whole group.
- B) establish goals yourself and communicate them clearly to the group, outlining how they will be achieved.
- C) share a broader vision for the project and let the group set specific goals that align with that vision.

4. How do you prefer to motivate your classmates during a group activity?
- A) By asking for their opinions and making sure everyone feels included
- B) By providing clear rules and giving direct instructions on what needs to be done
- C) By sharing your enthusiasm and encouraging everyone to work towards a shared vision

5. When faced with a tight deadline for a group assignment, you
- A) call a meeting to brainstorm solutions and get everyone's input on how to meet the deadline.
- B) take charge, delegate tasks based on everyone's strengths, and monitor progress closely.
- C) inspire your team with your vision of success and encourage them to work passionately towards completing the project.

6. How do you handle feedback from your peers about your leadership?
- A) Listen carefully and discuss how to incorporate their feedback into your leadership approach.
- B) Consider their feedback but make the final decision based on what you think is best.
- C) Use their feedback to refine your vision and motivate the group to achieve it.

7. How do you approach creating a group plan for a class presentation?
- A) Collaborate with everyone to come up with a detailed plan that incorporates everyone's ideas and strengths.
- B) Outline the plan yourself and assign roles based on each person's skills and the presentation requirements.
- C) Present a vision for the presentation and let the group develop the plan and work on their parts creatively.

8. When managing a group discussion, you
- ○ A) ensure that everyone has the opportunity to speak and contribute their ideas.
- ○ B) guide the discussion with clear objectives and keep it focused on the main topic.
- ○ C) drive the discussion with your ideas and encourage creative thinking to explore new possibilities.

Results

- **Mostly As: Democratic Leader**

Democratic leaders value the input of others and believe that decisions should be made together. You prefer being in spaces where everyone's ideas are respected and considered. This style is perfect for situations where group cohesion and collective decision-making are key.

- **Mostly Bs: Autocratic Leader**

Autocratic leaders are effective in situations requiring clear direction and quick decisions. You are decisive and efficient, often managing tasks and delegating responsibilities to ensure things are done properly. This style works well when quick, decisive action is needed or when there's a clear path that needs to be followed.

- **Mostly Cs: Transformational Leader**

Transformational leaders focus on creating a compelling vision and encouraging innovation and growth. You excel at motivating your team to embrace new ideas and work toward achieving a shared goal. This style is particularly effective in driving change and fostering a positive and dynamic team environment.

 Activity 2: Strengths and Weaknesses of Leaders

There are no such things as "perfect leaders." Each leadership style comes with its unique set of strengths and weaknesses. In this activity, you are required to browse through the internet and find three leaders who display the three leadership styles we explored in the previous activity: democratic, autocratic, and transformational leadership. These could be leaders in the business world, political world, or for social and environmental change. Provide a brief historical background about the leader, identify their leadership style and a list of leadership traits they possess, and then write a list of strengths and weaknesses they might have based on their leadership style.

Activity 3: Matching Leadership Traits With Critical Issues

The cool thing about discovering your leadership traits is that it helps you figure out how you can shine in team projects. For instance, if you're all about brainstorming and teamwork, you might be the one who gets team members to share their ideas and makes sure everyone's voice is heard when making decisions.

In this activity, you need to match different leadership traits with common group problems that need specific traits to solve them. Next to each number, write down the most suitable letter. Feel free to team up with other classmates to tackle this challenge together.

Common Group Problems	Leadership Traits
A. Some team members are not showing interest or putting effort into the project.	1. Encouraging
B. Team members are debating over whose ideas are right and whose ideas are wrong.	2. Organized
C. The team is falling behind on their schedule and might miss the deadline.	3. Decisive
D. Several team members feel as though nobody is listening to them.	4. Empathetic
E. Some team members are working harder than others.	5. Creative
F. Team members are not sharing information with each other effectively.	6. Reliable
G. Team members have two options but are confused about which one to go with.	7. Patient

Common Group Problems	Leadership Traits
H. New information has just been revealed which requires the team to change their plan.	8. Assertive
I. The team is distracted and not working efficiently to achieve their goals.	9. Adaptable
J. Secret animosity and hurt feelings are preventing the team from making progress.	10. Collaborative

A.

B.

C.

D.

E.

F.

G.

H.

I.

J.

Activity 4: The Elevator Pitch Challenge

One of the most powerful tools for a leader is their voice. To share their ideas and inspire others, they need to speak persuasively. Persuasion is all about convincing someone to believe in something and take action. This can be done by using facts, sharing benefits, showing real results, or appealing to the other person's interests.

Try the Elevator Pitch Challenge! This is a fun game you can play in groups of 4-5. Each person will prepare a short 2-minute speech about their favorite meal and then present it to the group. After each speech, the group members will score it out of 10 (for a total score out of 40-50) based on how persuasive it is. The goal is to convince everyone that your favorite meal is the best. When scoring, be honest and unbiased and note how many persuasive techniques were used.

 ## Activity 5: Decision-Making Made Easy

Being indecisive means delaying making a choice even when you have the information needed to take action. The longer you delay making a choice, the harder it becomes to commit to a plan. On the other hand, making snap decisions without taking the time to weigh the pros and cons might lead to mistakes and regrettable actions.

Ever had a decision that left you feeling confused or anxious? Let's tackle that indecisiveness head-on and learn to make responsible choices! Think about that recent decision and try this step-by-step process to see what you could've done differently:

1. What exactly is the challenge you are facing? Write it down.

_____

_____

_____

_____

_____

_____

_____

_____

_____

2. What areas of your life does this challenge impact? For instance, does it impact your focus or performance at school? Does it impact your friendships? Could it potentially affect your mental and physical health?

_____

_____

_____

_____

_____

_____

_____

_____

3. What will happen if you don't find a solution for this challenge? Look forward into the future, maybe 6-12 months down the line, and describe how the impacted areas of your life will look if nothing gets resolved.

_____

_____

_____

_____

_____

_____

_____

_____

_____

_____

4. Brainstorm the type of information you need to address this challenge. This could include advice from a teacher, learning materials, the school calendar and timetable, or certain skills or knowledge about the issue.

_____

_____

_____

_____

_____

_____

_____

_____

5. Gather the relevant information you need. This step can take a few days or up to several weeks, especially if you need to speak to someone face-to-face. Be patient with yourself while gathering information because it will help you with the next step, which is to think of potential solutions.

_____

_____

_____

_____

_____

_____

_____

_____

_____

_____

6. Once you have read through and analyzed all of the information, list all of the possible solutions. Don't think too hard about what you write. You can always come back and edit your ideas.

_____

_____

_____

_____

_____

_____

_____

_____

_____

7. Identify three solutions that are better than the rest and write out pros and cons for each of them.

_____

_____

_____

_____

_____

_____

_____

_____

_____

_____

_____

_____

_____

8. 1. Based on your pros and cons list, select two solutions that seem to be the most realistic and achievable solutions. Write out an action plan for each solution that involves five steps. The action steps should be simple tasks that you can start performing now.

_____

_____

_____

_____

_____

_____

_____

_____

9. Decide on which solution you are going to test first. Go through the action steps and journal about your experience along the way, such as what obstacles or opportunities you run into. If the first solution doesn't get you the results you need, turn to the alternative solution.

_____

_____

_____

_____

_____

_____

_____

_____

_____

_____

_____

Activity 6: Buy My Product

Negotiation is a discussion where two or more people aim to reach an agreement by finding common ground to satisfy everyone.

In this activity, your teacher will divide the class into sellers and buyers. Sellers will pretend to sell a product (real products like a cell phone or imaginary products like tickets to a football game) to buyers. Each group has 10 minutes to prepare. Sellers should highlight key features and selling points, while buyers should decide what they want and prepare tough questions.

After prep time, sellers and buyers will pair up for a 5-minute pitch session. Sellers will note any sales, then switch partners and pitch again for another 5 minutes. This process will repeat for 3-5 rounds, depending on time. In the end, sellers will tally their sales and share which negotiation tactics were most effective in convincing buyers.

 ## Activity 7: Reflecting on Your Role Models

Role models are people who you know personally or who you watch on TV, who inspire you to become a better person. Their positive energy, beliefs, and behaviors motivate you to learn certain skills, start hobbies, or participate in social causes. For this activity, you are required to identify one role model and prepare a speech about them. While writing your speech, explore questions such as:

1. What is their background? How did their background influence their personality and dreams?
2. What qualities do they display that you admire? In what ways are their qualities useful in their lives?
3. What inspiring words or advice have they shared that have encouraged you?
4. What are the similarities you see between you and your role model? Also, how are you both different?
5. What specific skills, hobbies, or goals have you started (or plan on starting) because of their positive influence?

 ## Activity 8: Task Delegation

During busy periods of your life, when you are overwhelmed by the demands and responsibilities placed on you, delegating tasks to your close friends and family can help you relieve stress and feel supported. Task delegation involves assigning someone you know and trust a task that you cannot fit into your schedule so that you can reduce your workload and get the support you need.

Below, you will find a list of common tasks you might deal with and flash cards with lists of people whom you know and trust. Go through the list of tasks and assign each one under the name of the person who could help with that task. Think about what each person is good at and how available they are when deciding who to ask for help.

Keep sorting until every task has been matched with someone who can take it on. You can cut out the flash cards and keep them somewhere safe for easy reference.

Task List
1. *Organizing a study schedule*
2. *Preparing a healthy meal*
3. *Helping with a science project*
4. *Managing a personal budget*
5. *Organizing a birthday party*
6. *Planning a weekend outing*
7. *Addressing learning challenges*
8. *Managing stress and anxiety*
9. *Improving social skills*
10. *Setting and achieving personal goals*
11. *Decluttering your bedroom*
12. *Preparing for high school*

Caregivers (i.e. Mom, Dad, Grandparents, Nannies, Family Friends)
Tasks they can help me with:

Friends (i.e. Classmates, Neighborhood Friends, Siblings, Cousins)

Tasks they can help me with:

Experts (i.e. Teachers, Special Needs Educators, Therapists, Doctors, Coaches)

Tasks they can help me with:

Activity 9: Win-Win Outcomes

The ideal outcome of a conflict is for parties to walk away feeling like winners. Win-win outcomes are creative solutions that take into consideration the needs and desires of both people. In this activity, you will practice coming up with win-win outcomes by studying the scenarios below and thinking about solutions that would satisfy both people.

Scenario: *You're working on a group project with a classmate but cannot agree on the layout of your presentation. You prefer creating a physical poster, while they prefer creating a slideshow. Suggest a win-win outcome.*

_____

_____

_____

_____

_____

_____

_____

_____

_____

_____

_____

_____

_____

_____

_____

_____

_____

_____

Scenario: *Your parents expect you to complete house chores every day, but you are normally tired when coming back from school. How can you negotiate a schedule that works for both of you? Suggest a win-win outcome.*

_____

_____

_____

_____

_____

_____

_____

_____

_____

Scenario: *You're trying to decide between two career paths: pursuing a technical field or a creative field. Your career counselor is recommending the technical field based on job market trends, but you are passionate about the creative field. How can you explore both career options and find a balance between market trends and personal passion? Suggest a win-win outcome.*

_____

_____

_____

_____

_____

_____

_____

_____

_____

_____

Activity 10: Inspiration Station

Everybody needs motivation to keep going. Effective leaders know how to motivate others through their caring words and actions. You can practice motivating your classmates by creating an inspiration station in groups of 3-4.

An inspiration station is simply a poster with various positive elements and details such as cool quotes, helpful tips, and coping strategies that uplift those around you. Choose a theme for your poster, like "Eighth Grade Survival Skills" or "Self-Care and Self-Love Practices" to help you focus on a specific inspiration. Use a variety of pens, markers, paints, magazine cutouts, decorations, and anything else that can make your poster eye-catching. Lastly, find a good spot to hang your poster in the classroom.

Activity 11: Setting a Positive Example

You have the ability to positively influence your friends and classmates through your words and actions. Whether you are aware of it or not, someone is always watching how you solve problems or treat other people and is taking notes. This activity will help you reflect on the good influence you have and how it benefits those around you.

For starters, write down three recent situations where you acted in a positive way, such as showing kindness, standing up for someone, assisting someone with schoolwork, or contributing to a group project. Describe what happened and how your actions made a difference.

_____

_____

_____

_____

_____

_____

_____

_____

_____

From each situation, identify a positive quality you displayed such as courage, honesty, patience, or leadership. Write the quality on a sticky note and place it on the whiteboard. Eventually, the whiteboard should be populated with many sticky notes highlighting positive qualities that each student has displayed. As a class, discuss how being a positive influence contributes to making a difference in the classroom and within the community.

 ## Activity 12: Pitch Perfect Presentation

Standing in front of the class to give a speech can be nerve-racking, but with the right public speaking skills, you can project confidence even if you're feeling anxious. To ace your presentation, team up in groups of three and pick a topic that everyone is excited about and can talk about for three minutes.

First, brainstorm and research your topic, then come up with nine key points to cover. Each person in your group will take three points and present them during their minute of speaking. Structure your talk with a clear introduction, body, and conclusion, and focus on these key public speaking skills:

- **Articulation:** *Speak clearly so everyone understands you.*
- **Engagement:** *Keep your audience interested with your energy and enthusiasm.*
- **Body language:** *Use gestures and maintain eye contact to make your points more impactful.*

Practice your presentation a few times as a group and give each other constructive feedback to improve. After all the presentations, your teacher will offer additional feedback on what went well and what could be even better.

 ## Activity 13: Checkpoint Mapping

Long-term goals can take 6-12 months or even longer to achieve, and keeping yourself motivated along the way is key. A great way to stay on track is by creating a "checkpoint map"–basically, a visual guide to help you track your progress and stay excited about your goal. Here's how to make one:

1. *Think about something big you want to achieve. It could be improving your grades, applying to a high school, or learning a new skill.*
2. *Figure out how long it will take to reach your goal. Is it a 6-month plan or something that will take over a year? Be specific with your timeline.*
3. *Break down your goal into major milestones. Write these checkpoints down and estimate how much time it will take to reach each one.*
4. *Add your checkpoints to a calendar and set reminders a few days before each one. This way, you can prepare and make sure you're on track.*
5. *If you're getting close to a checkpoint but need more time to complete smaller tasks, don't worry –just push the checkpoint date back by a week or so to catch up.*

Activity 14: Combating Procrastination on Smaller Tasks

In the last activity, you broke down your big goal into smaller checkpoints. Now, identify the smaller tasks needed to reach each checkpoint. Procrastination often happens with these small, ongoing tasks. **Here's how to stay on track:**

1. *Write down each checkpoint and the smaller tasks needed. For example, if a checkpoint is researching high schools, a task might be making a list of school criteria.*
2. *Note whether each task is a one-time activity or needs to be done regularly. Creating your criteria might be a one-time task, while applying to schools could be ongoing.*
3. *Estimate how long each task will take and decide when to do it. For instance, if a task takes 30 minutes, plan to complete it before school, in the afternoon, or evening.*
4. *Write a summary of each task on your calendar. For example: "Create high school criteria on Thursday, 4:00 p.m. to 5:00 p.m."*
5. *Ensure each task is achievable with your resources and time. Adjust as needed to stay on track.*

Activity 15: The Interview Coach

You have been hired by a young job candidate to coach them as they prepare for their first job interview. Since they haven't done this before, they need tips on how to behave professionally and make a good impression in front of the interviewer. Create a helpful guideline of positive and negative behaviors that could impact their performance. Consider factors such as:

- *dress code and physical appearance*
- *punctuality and time management*
- *greetings and introductions*
- *body language*
- *communication skills*
- *asking questions and answering questions*

Activity 16: Exploring Career Paths

Eighth grade is a great time to start thinking about careers you might love and excel at. It can feel overwhelming with so many options out there, but a good place to start is by looking at paths that spark your interest or match your personality. For this activity, you can choose to work solo or team up with a classmate. Your task is to research a career path that sounds cool but that you haven't looked into before.

Here are some sectors to consider:
- *Healthcare*

- *Education*
- *Public Service and Law*
- *Arts and Entertainment*
- *Science and Engineering*
- *Technology and Digital Media*
- *Construction and Architecture*
- *Environmental and Agriculture*
- *Business and Finance*

Once you've chosen a career, research it thoroughly and fill out the worksheet at the end of the chapter on the page titled "Exploring Career Paths." After that, create a slideshow presentation to share your findings with the class.

Activity 17: Matching Career Choices With Values

Your values are the beliefs and qualities that really matter to you. When your career choices match your values, you're more likely to find work that feels meaningful and motivating. This doesn't mean it won't be tough sometimes, but having a sense of purpose can keep you going even when things get challenging.

For this activity, you'll need to identify five values and brainstorm professions that align with at least three of them. Think about how these jobs promote those values, like offering a good work-life balance, giving you the freedom to work from home or set your own hours, allowing you to become wealthy over time, or providing opportunities for leadership.

Use these questions to help you find careers that match your values:

1. What activities or subjects make you feel excited and fulfilled? Consider hobbies, school subjects, or extracurricular activities that you enjoy.

_____

_____

_____

_____

_____

_____

_____

_____

_____

_____

_____

_____

_____

_____

_____

_____

2. What qualities do you admire in others? Think about traits you look up to in friends, family members, or role models.

_____

_____

_____

_____

_____

_____

_____

_____

_____

_____

3. When have you felt proudest of yourself? Reflect on moments where you felt a strong sense of accomplishment and ask yourself why.

_____

_____

_____

_____

_____

_____

_____

_____

_____

4. What aspects of your current or past experiences have you found most rewarding? Identify what made those experiences meaningful to you.

_____

_____

_____

_____

_____

_____

_____

_____

_____

_____

_____

_____

_____

5. What would you stand up for or defend passionately? Consider causes or principles you believe in deeply.

_____

_____

_____

_____

_____

_____

_____

6. What careers align with the activities or subjects that make you feel excited and fulfilled? Match your interests with potential professions that incorporate those activities.

_____

_____

_____

_____

_____

_____

_____

_____

_____

_____

_____

_____

7. Which professions embody the qualities you admire in others? Look for careers where these traits are essential or highly valued.

_____

_____

_____

_____

_____

_____

_____

_____

_____

_____

8. What jobs would allow you to experience the same sense of pride and accomplishment you've felt in the past? Identify professions that offer similar rewarding experiences.

_____

_____

_____

_____

_____

_____

_____

_____

_____

_____

_____

_____

_____

9. Which careers offer opportunities that align with the aspects you find most rewarding? Consider jobs that provide similar benefits and satisfactions.

_____

_____

_____

_____

_____

_____

_____

_____

10. What professions would let you stand up for or promote the causes or principles you are passionate about? Look for roles that allow you to advocate for or work towards these values.

_____

_____

_____

_____

_____

_____

_____

_____

_____

_____

_____

_____

Activity 18: Interviewing Professionals

Another way to learn more about a specific career path is to interview an expert who has worked in that field or position for several years. They would likely have the skills, knowledge, and experience needed to give you a full picture of what you can look forward to.

Your task for this activity is to choose a profession that interests you and find someone, preferably in your close network of friends and family, who performs that job. Create 10 unique interview questions to ask them about various aspects of their job, including the opportunities and challenges. Use the insights gathered from your interview to provide your teacher with a comprehensive overview of the career field, its pros and cons, and what you need to prepare in high school to increase your chances of entering the field.

 ## Activity 19: Resumé Writing

A resumé is your personal highlight reel, showcasing who you are and what you can do to future employers or schools. It helps you make a great first impression and demonstrates why you're the right fit for the role or program.

Essential elements for every resumé include:

- **Contact information:** *Name, phone number, and email.*
- **Summary:** *Brief statement about your goals and what you aim to achieve.*
- **Education:** *School name, grade, and any honors or awards.*
- **Experience:** *Jobs, volunteer work, internships, or significant projects.*
- **Skills:** *Abilities like teamwork, communication, and problem-solving.*
- **Interests/Hobbies:** *Extracurricular activities or personal interests that highlight your personality and strengths.*

Use the resumé template in the My Resumé section at the end of the chapter to fill in these details. Choose a template you like on a site like Canva, enter your information, and ensure it looks neat and professional. Save your resumé as a PDF for easy sharing and print a copy to submit to your teacher.

 ## Activity 20: Understanding Basic Financial Concepts

Part of growing up is learning about money-not just how to make it, but also how to use, multiply, and manage it. Basic financial concepts like savings, expenses, debt, and investments can teach you how to use money responsibly and plan for the future. For this activity, you'll team up in groups of 4-5 to look into a financial concept of your choice.

Choose one financial concept from the list below:

- *Savings*
- *Expenses*
- *Debt*
- *Investments*
- *Budgeting*
- *Credit*
- *Financial Planning*

Break down your chosen concept into key topics (e.g., definition, real-life application, benefits and drawbacks). Assign each group member one topic to research so that each of you can gather information from reliable sources and combine your findings into a cohesive project. Present your project to the class and be ready to answer questions and discuss your research.

Activity 21: Creating Financial Goals

Financial goals are basically the targets you set to manage your money for the stuff you want or need. Whether you're saving up for the latest sneakers or planning for college, the process is pretty much the same.

Here's a simple way to nail your financial goals:

1. Write down a goal you would like to save up for. It could be something fun like a new game or something important like sports equipment, a special trip, or even college.

_____

_____

_____

_____

_____

_____

_____

_____

_____

2. Figure out if it's a short-term goal (like saving up in the next 6 months), a medium-term goal (within 6-12 months), or a long-term goal (1-5 years).

_____

_____

_____

_____

_____

_____

_____

_____

_____

_____

3. Make your financial goal SMART by defining the specifics, measurement criteria, achievability, relevance, and time frame. Here are a few questions to guide you:

   A. *What exactly do you want to achieve?*
   B. *How will you track your progress? What key measurements will you use?*
   C. *Do you have the skills and tools required to start working on your goal?*
   D. *Does your goal align with your interests, beliefs, and passions?*
   E. *Have you set a deadline to achieve your goal?*

_____

_____

_____

_____

_____

_____

_____

_____

_____

_____

_____

_____

_____

_____

_____

_____

_____

_____

4. Team up with 3-4 classmates and share your goals with each other. Give and receive feedback on potential challenges and strategies. After discussing the feedback, adjust your goals to implement the advice you were given, then take action!

_____

_____

_____

_____

_____

_____

_____

_____

_____

_____

_____

Activity 22: Creating a Personal Budget

In the last activity, you set a financial goal. To achieve it, you'll need to adjust your money management. This activity will help you create a personal budget to track your monthly spending and savings. **Here's how to get started:**

1. Use the My Personal Budget sheet or a budgeting app to input your income and expenses.
2. Determine what percentage of your leftover money you'll save for your goal. For example, save 60% and spend 40%.
3. If you're spending more than you earn, review your expenses and find areas to cut back.
4. Record your transactions monthly and adjust your budget as needed to stay on track.

 Activity 23: Personal SWOT Analysis

A SWOT analysis is a tool that helps you look at all sides of a situation by breaking it down into strengths, weaknesses, opportunities, and threats. It's like a pros and cons list, but more detailed. Companies use SWOT analyses when they're making big decisions, but you can use them too for important choices in your life.

Here's a breakdown of the acronym SWOT:

1. **Strengths:** What you're good at and what resources you have
2. **Weaknesses:** Areas where you're lacking or things that might hold you back
3. **Opportunities:** External factors that you can take advantage of
4. **Threats:** External factors that might cause problems

Think about a big decision you need to make soon. It could be joining a new club, starting a small business, choosing elective courses, planning a school project, or considering a summer job. Turn to the Personal SWOT Analysis template at the end of the chapter and fill it out. Based on your SWOT analysis, decide what you're going to do (or how you are going to adjust your plan).

 Activity 24: Building a Personal Brand

You've likely heard of social media influencers who use their online presence to showcase their talents and build a personal brand. Their charm and unique skills draw us in, as they've crafted an identity that makes them recognizable and relatable.

You don't need to be an influencer to benefit from a personal brand. It can help you stand out in job interviews, leverage your strengths for new opportunities, and make a memorable impression on others. Grab a pen and follow these steps to create your own unique personal brand:

1. List your top skills, talents, and hobbies. Mention things that make you stand out from the crowd.

_____

_____

_____

_____

_____

_____

_____

_____

2. What compliments do you receive often from others? Mention the recurring positive feedback you get.

_____

_____

_____

_____

_____

_____

_____

_____

_____

_____

_____

_____

3. What positive impact do you aspire to make in the world? How do you plan on using your skills, talents, and hobbies to put smiles on people's faces?

_____

_____

_____

_____

_____

_____

_____

_____

_____

_____

4. How do you desire people to feel when they interact with you? What thoughts and emotions do you want them to have?

_____

_____

_____

_____

_____

_____

_____

_____

_____

_____

_____

_____

Use the information gathered from the questions above to create a vision board. Look for magazine or digital images that reflect the essence of your brand, who you are, and the positive difference you aspire to make in the world. Cut the images out and glue them on the page, creating a collage. While you are busy with the activity, think about what inspires you and where you see yourself in the future.

 ## Activity 25: Identifying Community Needs

Communities are groups of people who share common goals, values, and interests. We all belong to different communities, like our families, neighborhoods, schools, social clubs, and religious groups. By figuring out what our communities need and working to meet those needs, we can make a big difference in our lives and the lives of others.

Here's your mission:
1. Pick a community you're part of, such as your family, school, or neighborhood.
2. Think about what your community needs but isn't getting. For example, what problems do people in your community face? What could make your community stronger?
3. Rank your list from the most urgent and impactful to the least. Pick one of your top three needs to focus on.
4. Make your goal SMART. For example, If litter is a big issue in your neighborhood, a SMART goal could be, "To organize a weekly neighborhood cleanup event for the next three months to improve the cleanliness and appearance of my neighborhood."
5. To keep yourself on track, plan out the steps you need to take. Ask yourself:
   - A. What actions are needed to achieve the goal?
   - B. What resources (time, materials, people) are needed?
   - C. When will each step be completed?
   - D. Who will be responsible for each step?

 ## Activity 26: Planning a Donation Drive

A donation drive is a planned collection of items like food, clothing, and books to support those in need, such as vulnerable people or animals. It typically supports causes like animal rights, children's education, or homelessness. In this activity, you'll learn how to plan a donation drive so that you can be organized and confident in launching a drive for a cause you care about. Follow the steps outlined below to start the planning process!

1. Pick a cause that aligns with your interests and values. It's important to feel deeply connected to the cause so that you stay motivated throughout.

_____

_____

_____

_____

_____

_____

_____

_____

_____

2. Find a local organization that advocates for the cause. Go onto their website and read up about their initiatives and what type of problems they are solving. You can even call the organization to find out what collection items they need.

_____

_____

_____

_____

_____

_____

_____

_____

_____

_____

_____

_____

3. Think about the finer details of your drive, such as:

- *What are your drive's goals and objectives?*
- *What items will you collect? Where will you store your collected items? How will you keep a record of everything you have collected?*
- *Who will you ask for donations? How will you make them aware of your drive?*
- *Is it going to be a physical drive where you interact with people or an online drive where you share a link that people can follow?*
- *How long will your drive be? Why do you need that much time?*
- *What resources will you need? For example, will you need a tent, posters, T-shirts, or money to rent a stand in a market?*
- *Who will help you put together the drive? What specific duties will you assign to each person?*

_____

_____

_____

_____

_____

_____

_____

_____

_____

_____

_____

_____

_____

_____

_____

_____

Activity 27: Volunteering Opportunities

For many students, college is the top choice after school, but if you're considering a gap year or exploring alternatives to higher education, volunteering can be a great option. Volunteering offers local and international programs through charitable organizations, allowing you to support underserved communities while gaining valuable skills and experiences.

Your task is to research five volunteering opportunities (local, international, or both) suited for young people. Imagine you're planning a year of charitable work and need to find programs that align with your goals. For each opportunity, answer the following:

1. What is the program, and what cause does it support?
2. What activities and opportunities does it offer?
3. When does it start, and how long does it last?
4. Who can participate, and what are the requirements? Are there application forms?
5. Where is the program based, how do you get there, and what type of accommodation is provided?
6. What is the cost to participate? How much will you need for your trip, and what expenses are covered by the program?

 ## Activity 28: Preparing for High School and Beyond

Be honest: How do you feel about transitioning to high school? Are you prepared? Perhaps you are feeling a combination of excitement and nervousness about what the next phase of your education has in store for you.

To ensure that you are organized and have thought about everything you need to make high school a success, go through the Thriving in High School checklist provided at the end of the chapter. Don't worry if you haven't completed many of the items listed on the checklist. Treat them as short-term goals that you can start working on, one at a time, from today!

 ## Activity 29: Drafting Your Mission Statement

Being in eighth grade is an exciting time of your life. You have just entered teenagehood and are discovering who you are and what type of opportunities you want to strive for at school and in your personal life. Now is the best time to draft a mission statement to reflect on the person you desire to become and the meaningful impact you want to make in the world.

Complete the following prompts to brainstorm various aspects of your mission statement.

I want to be a young person who...

_____
_____
_____
_____
_____
_____
_____
_____
_____

The most important values in my life are...

_____
_____
_____
_____
_____
_____
_____
_____
_____
_____
_____
_____
_____

My personal strengths and the talents that set me apart are...

_____

_____

_____

_____

_____

_____

_____

_____

_____

I will use my strengths and talents to improve my life by...

_____

_____

_____

_____

_____

_____

_____

_____

_____

_____

_____

_____

My short-term and long-term goals include...

_____

_____

_____

_____

_____

_____

_____

_____

When I face challenges toward my goals, I will keep myself motivated by...

_____

_____

_____

_____

_____

_____

_____

_____

_____

_____

_____

Success to me means...

_____
_____
_____
_____
_____
_____
_____
_____
_____
_____

When I graduate high school, I want to be remembered for...

_____
_____
_____
_____
_____
_____
_____
_____
_____
_____
_____
_____
_____
_____
_____

Exercise

Summarize your responses and follow the template below to draft your mission statement. (Replace the instructions written in square brackets with the information you have gathered from the prompts.)

I want to be a young person who [state your focus or purpose]. **I am guided by values such as** [list your key values such as integrity, creativity, and compassion]. **I use my strengths in** [mention specific skills or talents] **to** [describe how you apply them]. **My goals include** [outline your short-term and long-term goals]. **Despite challenges such as** [mention any obstacles], **I will** [explain how you plan to overcome them]. **To me, success means** [define what success looks like for you, such as achieving personal growth or making a difference]. **When I graduate from high school, I want to be remembered for** [state how you want to be remembered and the legacy you wish to leave].

Activity 30: Future Habits to Adopt Today

To become the best version of yourself, you will need to gradually work toward adopting better habits. Based on the personal mission statement you drafted in the previous activity, write down some habits that can help you achieve your mission.

Focus on small behavior adjustments that you can easily incorporate into your current routine. For example, if your mission is to improve your grades, you might write down habits like "review class notes every night" or "ask questions in class." Make sure your new habits are specific and clear. Instead of saying "Exercise more," try "Go for a 20-minute walk after school." Keep a simple chart to track how well you're sticking to your new habits.

_____

_____

_____

_____

_____

_____

_____

_____

_____

_____

_____

_____

_____

_____

_____

_____

_____

_____

_____

Being a leader means stepping up to tackle problems that others might overlook and working to make your school and community a better place. You have the strength and personality to be a confident leader and make a real impact on those around you. Keep in mind that setting goals and planning ahead are key to being prepared for what's coming and making smart choices. So, get ready to lead and make a difference!

Exploring Career Paths

Complete the career worksheet below to find out more about your chosen career path.

Part 1: Basic Information

In this section, you are required to provide general information about your selected career path.

Career Title

_____

_____

_____

Sector

_____

_____

_____

Job Description

_____

_____

_____

Average Starting Salary

_____

_____

_____

_____

Part 2: Education & Training

Go one step further and research the specific qualifications, certifications, training, and experience required to enter this career path.

Majors in High School (if applicable)

_____

_____

_____

_____

Minimum Level of Education Required (e.g., high school diploma or bachelor's degree)

_____

_____

_____

_____

Additional Training, Licenses, or Certifications

_____

_____

_____

_____

Typical Career Progression (e.g. junior, specialist, or managerial opportunities)

_____

_____

_____

_____

Part 3: Skills & Qualities

Explore the range of skills and personal qualities that are advantageous to have when entering this career path.

Key Skills

_____

_____

_____

_____

_____

_____

Personal Qualities

_____

_____

_____

_____

_____

_____

Part 4: Work Environment

Research the type of work conditions that are typical for your career path.

Work Setting

_____
_____
_____
_____

Typical Work Hours

_____
_____
_____
_____

Work-Life Balance

_____
_____
_____
_____

Potential Challenges

_____
_____
_____
_____

My Resumé

Fill out the resumé template below to ensure that you have the crucial information required on every resumé. Once complete, design your resumé using a free template on a graphic design website like Canva.

Contact Information

- *Name:* _____

- *Phone Number:* _____

- *Email:* _____

Summary
A brief statement about your goals and what you hope to achieve.

Example:
"A motivated and hardworking student aiming to leverage my skills and experiences in a dynamic learning environment. I seek opportunities to further develop my teamwork and leadership abilities."

Education

- *School Name:* _____

- *Grade:* _____

- *Honors/Awards:* _____

Example:
- *Springfield Middle School*
- *8th Grade*
- *Honor Roll (2023), Science Fair Winner (2022)*

Experience
List any jobs, volunteer work, internships, or significant projects.

Example:
- *Volunteer, Community Library, Summer 2023*
    - *Assisted with organizing events and managing book inventory*

- *Babysitter, Local Neighborhood, 2022-Present*
    - *Provided childcare for multiple families*

Skills

List personal skills like teamwork, communication, and problem-solving.

Example:
- *Teamwork*
- *Effective Communication*
- *Problem-Solving*
- *Time Management*

Interests/Hobbies:

Extracurricular activities or personal interests that show your personality and strengths.

Example:
- *Member of the school's Robotics Club*
- *Passionate about playing the guitar*
- *Enjoy reading science fiction books*
- *Active participant in school soccer team*

My Personal Budget

Use the budgeting template below to draft your monthly budget.

My Financial Goal

Monthly Target Required ($) _____

Tracking My Income and Expenses

Record your total monthly income and expenses below.

Monthly Income

Allowance: $_____

Money from Chores/Part-Time Job: $_____

Gifts or Other Income: $_____

Total Monthly Income: $_____

Monthly Expenses

Coffee/Drinks: $_____

Transport (e.g., bus fare, gas): $_____

Subscriptions (e.g., library, streaming): $_____

Printing/School Supplies: $_____

Outings with Friends: $_____

Hobbies/Activities: $_____

Takeout/Food: $_____

Other Expenses (specify): $_____

Total Monthly Expenses: $_____

Savings Allocation

Based on your set monthly target to achieve your financial goal, decide on how to distribute your money.

Percentage to save for goals (e.g., 60%): $_____

Percentage for personal spending (e.g., 40%): $_____

Notes and Adjustments

At the end of each month, take down a few notes on the changes that have occurred, such as the expenses that you have cut back on or increased allocation toward your goals. These notes help you keep track on how well your budgeting plan is working.

My Personal SWOT Analysis

Complete the SWOT analysis template below to assess the impact of the decision you are planning on making.

My Future Decision

Strengths

Think about what you are good at and what resources you have that can help you with your decision.
Examples: *personal skills, supportive network, available resources, past experiences.*

Weaknesses

Consider any limitations or challenges you might face internally. Examples: lack of experience, limited resources, personal habits, skill gaps.

Opportunities

Look at the external factors that could benefit your decision. [These factors make your decision worthwhile.] *Examples*: new trends, potential collaborations, supportive environment, emerging needs.

Threats

Think about the external factors that could pose challenges or risks. [These factors make your decision risky or disadvantageous.] *Examples*: competition, changing circumstances, financial risks, negative trends.

Reflection & Feedback

Reflect on your responses and comment on what you believe is best to do, now that you have gathered more information. How might you adjust your decision to make use of your strengths, find a way around your weaknesses, capitalize on opportunities being presented to you, and avoid threats as much as possible?

Thriving in High School

The following checklist will help you prepare mentally and academically for a successful high school experience. Check off items you have already done and set goals to work on those you still need to complete.

Immediate Tasks (Within Days)	Check (X)
Reflect on Middle School Experiences • Write down what you enjoyed and found challenging in middle school. • Identify skills and subjects you excelled in and areas where you want to improve.	
Set Personal Goals • Create a list of goals for high school, both academic and personal. • Include goals for grades, extracurricular activities, and social experiences.	
Organize Your Materials • Sort through and organize your school supplies, notebooks, and digital files. • Create a folder for important documents and information for high school.	

Talk to Your Guidance Counselor	
• Schedule a meeting with your school counselor to discuss your high school transition. • Ask about course selection, extracurriculars, and any concerns you might have.	

Short-Term Tasks (Within Weeks)	Check (X)
Visit Your Future High School • If possible, attend an orientation or tour your high school to familiarize yourself with the campus. • Learn the school layout, including where classes, the cafeteria, and the library are located.	
Learn About High School Course Requirements • Review the high school curriculum and graduation requirements. • Choose elective courses and think about any advanced or specialized classes you might want to take.	
Develop Time Management Skills • Practice using a planner or digital calendar to manage your time and assignments. • Start planning your daily and weekly schedule, including homework, activities, and relaxation time.	

Explore Extracurricular Activities • Research clubs, sports, and other extracurriculars that are offered at your high school. • Decide which activities you're interested in and find ways to get involved.	
Build Study Habits • Develop a study routine that works for you and stick to it. • Experiment with different study techniques to find what helps you retain information best.	

Long-Term Tasks (Within Months)	Check (X)
Enhance Academic Skills • *Review key subjects you will need for high school, such as math, science, and language arts.* • *Consider summer courses or tutoring if you want to strengthen specific skills.*	
Develop Social Skills • *Practice communication and interpersonal skills by joining groups or participating in team activities.* • *Learn how to handle peer pressure and maintain healthy relationships.*	
Plan for High School Supplies • *Make a list of supplies you will need for high school, such as textbooks, notebooks, and a backpack.* • *Purchase or gather these supplies ahead of time to avoid last-minute shopping.*	

Prepare for New Responsibilities • *Understand that high school will come with more responsibilities and independence.* • *Talk to older siblings or friends about their experiences and tips for managing responsibilities.*	
Create a Support Network • *Identify family members, friends, and mentors who can support you throughout high school.* • *Discuss your goals and expectations with them and ask for their advice and support.*	

Conclusion

Reflect on the Journey

Risk more than others think is safe. Care more than others think is wise. Dream more than others think is practical. Expect more than others think is possible.

- Claude T. Bissell

Over the course of three inspiring and stimulating chapters, we have examined the five core SEL competencies: self-management, social awareness, self-awareness, relationship skills, and responsible decision-making. The themes for each chapter reflected the social and emotional needs of students at their various educational levels. Through engaging and collaborative activities, students have taken the opportunity to learn and enforce these skills in their personal and academic lives, allowing them to emerge at the end of the workbook more empowered than they were at the beginning.

Nevertheless, the journey to honing SEL skills doesn't end here. Students are encouraged to practice their grade-level activities more than once, using different examples and scenarios to apply the skills to their everyday life situations. Beyond that, students can also challenge themselves by exploring additional activities at higher grade levels. The aim is not for them to be graded on these additional activities, but instead to deepen their understanding of social contexts and to practice using different tools.

Looking Ahead: Applying SEL in Everyday Life

Reflecting on previous activities is another way to continue learning and growing. Ask students to refer back to strategies taught in previous activities to solve problems inside and outside of the classroom. You are also welcome to modify some of the activities included in this workbook and incorporate them as part of your lesson plans so that students are re-exposed to them.

Note-taking and journaling are also great techniques that students can practice to keep track of their progress and goals and take responsibility for their learning. Make these techniques a norm in your classroom by including elements of both in everyday classwork.

SEL skills are not supposed to be practiced once or in one particular setting. They are designed to be integrated into students' lives, positively impacting their thoughts, emotions, and behaviors in various settings. Show your students how these five competencies can help to solve multiple social problems and boost their confidence in engaging with people from all walks of life.

Equipped with SEL skills, you can rest assured that your wonderful students can overcome the unpredictable conditions of school and home life. Do your part in helping them stay open-minded, curious, and proactive in self-improvement.

If you have found the activities and insights in this workbook helpful, we'd love to hear from you! Please take a moment to leave a comment and share your experience on the book's Amazon page under "Reviews." Your feedback not only helps us improve but also guides other educators in discovering the valuable learning opportunities this workbook offers.

About the Author

Richard Bass

Richard Bass is a well-established author with extensive knowledge and background on children's disabilities. Richard has also experienced first-hand many children and teens who deal with depression and anxiety. He enjoys researching techniques and ideas to better serve students, as well as guiding parents on how to understand and lead their children to success.

Richard wants to share his experience, research, and practices through his writing, as it has proven successful for many parents and students.

Richard feels there is a need for parents and others around the child to fully understand the disability or the mental health of the child. He hopes that with his writing people will be more understanding of children going through these issues.

Richard Bass has been in education for over a decade and holds a bachelor's and master's degree in education as well as several certifications including Special Education K-12, and Educational Administration.

Whenever Richard is not working, reading, or writing he likes to travel with his family to learn about different cultures as well as get ideas from all around about the upbringing of children especially those with disabilities. Richard also researches and learns about different educational systems around the world.

Richard participates in several online groups where parents, educators, doctors, and psychologist share their success with children with disabilities. Richard is in the process of growing a Meta group where further discussion about his books and techniques could take place. Apart from online groups, he has also attended trainings regarding the upbringing of students with disabilities and has also led trainings in this area.

A Message from the Author

If you enjoyed the book and are interested on further updates or just a place to share your thoughts with other readers or myself, please join my Facebook group by scanning below!

If you would be interested on receiving a FREE Planner for kids PDF version, by signing up you will also receive exclusive notifications to when new content is released and will be able to receive it at a promotional price. Scan below to sign up!

Scan below to check out my content on You Tube and learn more about Neurodiversity!

References

- Adeyemi, E. (n.d.). How to help your child plan their future. Tutero. https://www.tutero.com.au/blog/how-to-help-your-child-plan-their-future

- Astray, T. (2020, March 19). Communication tool: Assertive confrontation and boundary setting with the DESO script. Tatiana Astray. https://www.tatianaastray.com/managing-relationships/2020/3/18/communication-tool-assertive-confrontation-and-boundary-setting-with-the-deso-script

- Athal, K. (2023, March 27). How to explain leadership to a kid. Times of India. https://timesofindia.indiatimes.com/blogs/krishna-athal/how-to-explain-leadership-to-a-kid/

- Birt, J. (2022, October 1). 15 types of questions (with definitions and examples). Indeed. https://www.indeed.com/career-advice/career-development/types-of-questions

- Bissell, C. T. (n.d.). Claude Thomas Bissell quotes. Goodreads. https://www.goodreads.com/quotes/247659-risk-more-than-others-think-is-safe-care-more-than

- Brennan, F. (2020, July 28). Six trust building activities for kids. All Pro Dad. https://www.allprodad.com/trust-activities-for-kids/

- CASEL. (n.d.). Fundamentals of SEL. https://casel.org/fundamentals-of-sel/

- Chambers, Y. (2018, April 27). Best guide for teaching kids the decision making process steps. Kiddie Matters. https://www.kiddiematters.com/problem-solving-activity-free-printable/

- Chloe. (2023, October 7). How to build self-awareness for kids: 10+ best practices. La Petite Ecole Ho Chi Minh. https://www.lpehochiminh.com/en/self-awareness-for-kids/

- Cipriano, C., Strambler, M. J., Naples, L. H., Ha, C., Kirk, M. A., Wood, M. E., Sehgal, K., Zieher, A. K., Eveleigh, A., McCarthy, M., Funaro, M., Ponnock, A., Chow, J. C., & Durlak, J. (2023, February 2). Stage 2 report: The state of the evidence for social and emotional learning: A contemporary meta-analysis of universal school-based SEL interventions. In OSF Preprints. https://doi.org/10.31219/osf.io/mk35u

- Cruze, R. (2024, January 9). 15 ways to teach kids about money. Ramsey Solutions. https://www.ramseysolutions.com/relationships/how-to-teach-kids-about-money

- Cummings, E. E. (n.d.). E. E. Cummings quotes. BrainyQuote. https://www.brainyquote.com/quotes/e_e_cummings_161592

- Cyberbullying. (n.d.). Nemours TeensHealth. https://kidshealth.org/en/teens/cyberbullying.html

- Durlak, J. A., Mahoney, J. L., & Boyle, A. E. (2022). What we know, and what we need to find out about universal, school-based social and emotional learning programs for children and adolescents: A review of meta-analyses and directions for future research. Psychological Bulletin, 148(11-12), 765-782. https://doi.org/10.1037/bul0000383
- Edwards, N. (2021, June 10). Children's activity: Life wheel assessments. Dandelion Training And Development. https://dandeliontraininganddevelopment.com/2021/06/childrens-activity-life-wheels/
- Eichar, D. (2022, November 16). How to plan a donation drive for your cause. 2MODA. https://www.2moda.com/blogs/blog/how-to-plan-a-donation-drive-for-your-cause
- Eidens, A. (2024, July 12). *31 kindness activities for kids*. Big Life Journal. https://biglifejournal.com/blogs/blog/kids-kindness-activities
- ElevatEd. (2021, May 20). *Famous young activists who made a difference in the world with their speeches*. 98th Percentile. https://www.98thpercentile.com/blog/motivational-speakers
- *Identifying your values and aligning them with your career*. (n.d.). Guild. https://www.guild.com/member-resources/identifying-your-values-and-aligning-them-with-your-career/
- Indeed Editorial Team. (2022, November 24). *What is persuasion? Definition, examples and how it works*. Indeed. https://in.indeed.com/career-advice/career-development/what-is-persuasion
- Kelly, K. (n.d.). *How to help your child understand body language*. Understood. https://www.understood.org/en/articles/at-a-glance-helping-your-child-understand-body-language
- Kenton, W. (2024, June 29). *How to perform a SWOT analysis*. Investopedia. https://www.investopedia.com/terms/s/swot.asp
- *Make s'mores with a solar oven!* (n.d.). NASA Climate Kids. https://climatekids.nasa.gov/smores/
- Mattingly, J. (2020, November 30). *Developing problem-solving skills for kids*. Kodable Education. https://www.kodable.com/learn/problem-solving-skills-for-kids
- The Mediation Center of the Coastal Empire. (n.d.). *All about peer mediation*. https://mediationsavannah.com/peer-mediation/
- Michaels, T. (2020, May 28). *Teach children about personal branding (why and how)*. Tolu Michaels. https://tolumichaels.com/teach-children-about-personal-branding/
- Miller, K. (2019, May 21). *Thirty-nine communication games and activities for kids and students*. Positive Psychology. https://positivepsychology.com/communication-activities-adults-students/
- Moore, D. (2023, July 19). *Igniting inspiration: How to inspire people*. Peregrine Global. https://peregrineglobal.com/how-to-inspire-people/
- Mullins, M. (n.d.). *Matty Mullins quotes*. Goodreads. https://www.goodreads.com/quotes/1005688-the-only-person-you-should-try-to-be-better-than
- Mydoh. (2021, December 22). *Budgeting for kids: How to make a budget for kids*. Mydoh. https://www.mydoh.ca/learn/money-101/money-basics/how-to-create-a-budget-for-kids-and-teens/

- Polevoi, L. (2023, September 6). *What are the 4 most common leadership styles?* The Alternative Board. https://www.thealternativeboard.com/blog/what-are-the-4-most-common-leadership-styles-
- Roosevelt, T. (n.d.). *Theodore Roosevelt quotes.* BrainyQuote. https://www.brainyquote.com/quotes/theodore_roosevelt_140484
- Smart, J. (2024, June 25). *40 problem solving techniques and activities to create effective solutions.* Session Lab. https://www.sessionlab.com/blog/problem-solving-techniques/
- Thurman, H. (n.d.). *Howard Thurman quotes.* Goodreads. https://www.goodreads.com/quotes/6273-don-t-ask-what-the-world-needs-ask-what-makes-you
- *What are SMART goals in education?* (n.d.). Twinkl. https://www.twinkl.co.za/teaching-wiki/smart-goals-in-education

Image References

- Burton, K. (2020, December 10). Cheerful diverse students sharing laptop while studying on street stairs [Image]. Pexels. https://www.pexels.com/photo/cheerful-diverse-students-sharing-laptop-while-studying-on-street-stairs-6147444/
- Danilyuk, P. (2021, May 6). A group of friends taking a selfie [Image]. Pexels. https://www.pexels.com/photo/a-group-of-friends-taking-a-selfie-7803659/
- Kampus Production. (2020, November 20). Young student making presentation to classmates and teacher [Image]. Pexels. https://www.pexels.com/photo/young-student-making-presentation-to-classmates-and-teacher-5940831/
- Krukau, Y. (2021, June 4). Man in gray sweater holding black digital table smiling [Image]. Pexels. https://www.pexels.com/photo/man-in-gray-sweater-holding-black-digital-table-smiling-8199596/
- OpenClipart-Vectors. (2013, October 16). Treasure map treasure hunt pirate treasure [Image]. Pixabay. https://pixabay.com/vectors/treasure-map-treasure-hunt-153425/
- Rimoldi, A. (2020, October 8). Men sitting at the park while having conversation [Image]. Pexels. https://www.pexels.com/photo/men-sitting-at-the-park-while-having-conversation-5554289/
- SagarArt. (2022, December 23). Black circle circle shape [Image]. Pixabay. https://pixabay.com/illustrations/black-circle-circle-shape-7669912/

Made in the USA
Coppell, TX
02 November 2024

39484992R00103